Critical Acclaim for the first book in the How It Works series, *PC/Computing How Computers Work* by Ron White

"A 'real' book, and quite a handsome one...The artwork, by Mr. Timothy Edward Downs, is striking and informative, and the text by Mr. White, executive editor of [*PC/Computing*], is very lucid."

—L.R. Shannon, *New York Times*

"...a magnificently seamless integration of text and graphics that makes the complicated physics of the personal computer seem as obvious as gravity. When a book really pleases you—and this one does—there's a tendency to gush, so let's put it this way: I haven't seen any better explanations written (including my own) of how a PC works and why."

—Larry Blasko, *The Associated Press*

"If you're curious but fear computerese might get in the way, this book's the answer...it's an accessible, informative introduction that spreads everything out for logical inspection. Readers will come away knowing not only what everything looks like but also what it does."

—Stephanie Zvirin, *Booklist*

"Read [*PC/Computing*] *How Computers Work,* to learn about the inner workings of the IBM and PC-compatible."

—Ronald Rosenberg, *Boston Globe*

"...the text in *How Computers Work* is remarkably free of jargon and distractions. Readers are left with a basic impression of how a particular component works; they're not overloaded with information they may never use or remember...For most PC users, the brief introduction to the subject of disk caching in *How Computers Work* is all they need to understand the basics behind the technology. This is a boon to readers who may have been totally stumped by a more technical description of the process, and who may have avoided the more indepth article. Whether you're new to computers or want a refresher course in the latest technology, *How Computers Work* offers a solid and colorful introduction."

—Gordon McComb, *Copley News Service*

"Computer users at all levels will enjoy and profit from this book."

—Don Mills, *Computing Now!*

"From mouse to CD-ROM, the treatment manages to convey 'how it works' without being simplistic or overly complex. A very good overview for those curious about how computers make their magic."

—*Reference & Research Book News*

HOW
SOFTWARE
WORKS

HOW
SOFTWARE
WORKS

RON WHITE

Illustrated by
PAMELA DRURY WATTENMAKER

Ziff-Davis Press
Emeryville, California

Senior Development Editor	Melinda E. Levine
Copy Editor	Janna Clark
Technical Reviewer	John Taschek
Project Coordinator	Kim Haglund
Proofreader	Cort Day
Cover Illustrator	Pamela Drury Wattenmaker
Cover Designer	Carrie English
Book Designer	Carrie English
Technical Illustrator	Pamela Drury Wattenmaker
Layout Artist	Bruce Lundquist
Digital Prepress Specialist	Joe Schneider
Word Processors	Howard Blechman, Cat Haglund, and Allison Levin
Indexer	Mark Kmetzko

Ziff-Davis Press books are produced on a Macintosh computer system with the following applications: FrameMaker®, Microsoft® Word, QuarkXPress®, Adobe Illustrator®, Adobe Photoshop®, Adobe Streamline™, MacLink®Plus, Aldus® FreeHand™, Collage Plus™.

Ziff-Davis Press
5903 Christie Avenue
Emeryville, CA 94608

ISBN 1-56276-133-1

Manufactured in the United States of America

10 9 8 7 6 5 4 3 2

**To Sue,
whose understanding
of how I work
is almost scary.**

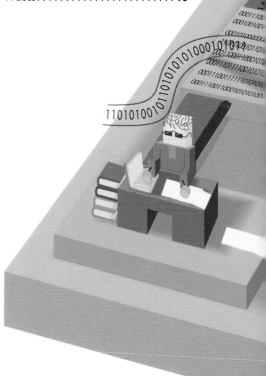

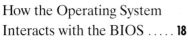

This book is the result of efforts by many people, and if it contains any mistakes, I'll happily take the fall for misinterpreting the information they provided.

PC/Computing Associate Editor Dylan Tweney and Assistant Editor Liesl La Grange did much of the actual research for this book. Without their help, I would never have been able to complete it on deadline—or at least as close to deadline as I came. Both were diligent and inventive in tracking down new sources of information, and I am extremely grateful for their work.

Among the people who gave of their time and knowledge are Jeff Bonar, Kraig Brockschmidt, Jon DeVaan, Brent Ethington, Dennis Foster, Ed Fries, Andreas Guralas, Manny Ko, Woody Leonhard, Miriam Liskin, Jim McNellis, Jim Millecam, Jeff Prosise, Alex Pryce, Steve Rimmer in his book *Supercharged Bitmapped Graphics*, Neil J. Rubenking, Gina Smith, Shelly Soffer, and Mike Troyan. John Taschek and Neil Rubenking read the book for technical errors and saved my skin more often than I like to remember.

At ZD Press, I'm grateful to Cindy Hudson for her unflagging enthusiasm for this project; to my editor, Melinda Levine, for making sense of what was too often hurried writing and for keeping me on track; to Janna Clark for doing more than simply correcting grammar and, instead, often smoothing out my tangled sentences; and to Kim Haglund, who often spotted logical inconsistencies in my original sketches. And I'm once again grateful to Ziff-Davis Executive Vice President and former *PC/Computing* Publisher Mike Edelhart, who kept insisting that the "How It Works" feature in *PC/C* was a natural for a book; this led to my previous book, *How Computers Work*, and then to this.

And I'm thankful more than I can express to Pamela Drury Wattenmaker, whose art work has transformed my crude sketches into beautiful, clear visual representations of the information this book tries to explain. The earlier *How Computers Work* was easier to illustrate in the sense that it was mostly about real objects you could hold in your hands and readily convert to illustrations. Software by its nature is abstract; there is nothing "real" to draw. When I explained to Pam my idea for personifying software with robots inspired by those in the movie *Silent Running*, she grasped instantly what needed to be done. And too often, I sent Pam sketches on which I had scrawled a note of apology because I couldn't imagine any robot representing a particular software function. She always came through with her own imaginative, appropriate creations.

Finally, I'm forever grateful for the understanding of my wife, Sue, who realized that completing this book meant long evenings and weekends during which I provided all the companionship of a pet rock. She has always provided the right encouragement and inspiration when my own ran dry.

Ron White
San Antonio

Sa-la-ga-doo-la Men-chic-ka Boo-la Bibbidi-Bobbidi-Boo. Put them together and what have you got? Bibbidi-Bobbidi-Boo.

—Walt Disney's *Cinderella*

For most people who've never before looked at any of the source code for computer software, that code is hardly more intelligible than the fairy godmother's incantation. Magic, of course, shouldn't be too simple. Simple things are rarely powerful, and software is one of the most powerful tools that the human race has created. But for many, it still is magic. You put a floppy disk into your PC, or you type the name of a program, or you point at a file with a mouse and click, and suddenly all these things begin to happen that those who lived before us might have described only as witchery. Beautiful color images and voices and sounds emanate from your PC. The software looks at a series of numbers and predicts what banana futures will be three months from now. You ask for information on a person, a country, or a date, and the software responds like a crystal ball. You ask the software to take you to a distant electronic bulletin board, and in seconds you're transported there as if you were sailing on a magic carpet.

As powerful and as full of abracadabra as software seems, it's possible for all of us to become sorcerer's apprentices. This book is not intended to make a software programmer of you, but even without learning all the arcane mysteries of program code, you can learn the fundamentals of how this magic works and how powerful it can be, and gain new respect for this magic and its creators. You will also be better able to use that aspect of the magic you have access to—the software, its words and images, that program code causes to materialize on your screen.

There has always been something a bit fearful about computers and software. Fear always accompanies something we don't understand. That's what this book is about: helping you to understand what your software is doing. And that's inevitably more complex than it is as described in these pages. I've taken the liberty of oversimplying in order to concentrate on the larger issues and to avoid the confusing minutiae of detail. Those who know better might spot an explanation that covers only one aspect of how some software function works. What can I say? I certainly won't argue that software isn't more complex and subtle, but I will argue that this book tells you what is most important to understand about that complex chemistry.

One vast oversimplification, however, is that I've limited my discussion to DOS and Windows-based software. For all the Mac enthusiasts out there, I can only say that, in principle, how their software works is fundamentally the same as how DOS PC-based programs work. But to avoid endless comparisons between DOS and Mac systems, I chose to concentrate only on the operating environment with which I'm most familiar.

All that said, I hope you find this information entertaining as well as useful. The study of software is a mental exercise more invigorating than any I've ever encountered. I hope you share my joy in the pure contemplation of the cleverness of programs and programmers.

HOW HARDWARE AND SOFTWARE WORK TOGETHER

CONTENTS

EVEN IF YOU'VE never touched a computer before, you've used software. Just as WordPerfect and Lotus 1-2-3 are software, so too are music recordings and videotapes. A recipe for Aunt Hattie's carrot cake, a dress pattern, and a telephone number are programs. A *program* is a set of instructions for an ordered series of actions. It may exist as a printout of computer code or as a recipe in a cookbook—any form that cannot be read directly by hardware. A person or machine has to perform the actions described in the program each time it's used. *Software* is a special form of a program; it's been recorded in some form—on a computer disk or on a videotape—so that the program doesn't have to be entered manually into the hardware each time it's used.

What programs and software have in common in all their forms is that they instruct a piece of hardware how to do something useful. A phonograph (or to be more contemporary, a CD player), a VCR, an oven and cookware, a sewing machine, and a telephone are all hardware. Hardware is a tangible object, a tool really, that sits there inert and useless until programming or software makes it come alive.

By itself, for example, a claw hammer is nothing more useful than a paperweight. But used by a carpenter, it can drive nails, pull out old nails, and even crack walnuts. The carpenter swinging the hammer is programming it on the fly.

Some hardware—your collection of cookware and stove, sewing machine, and telephone—require more complex on-the-fly human involvement. The processes of cooking, sewing, and calling Aunt Hattie to find out why your carrot cake isn't like hers are akin to the precise, ordered manual programming of the early days of personal computers. The first PCs were bought largely by hobbyists fascinated by the sheer idea of owning their own computers. Those PCs had neither a keyboard nor a monitor. Their owners programmed them through a tedious process of flipping switches in a precise order, and then read the results of their computer's labor from a pattern of lights on the front of the machine.

What those computer hobbyists did is comparable to what you often have to do when you use your microwave oven: You press buttons in a certain order to make the microwave work at a specific power level for a certain length of time. That's programming.

But if you press a button that's preset for microwave popcorn, then you're using software—a preconfigured set of programming instructions that, in this case, are recorded permanently in a microchip inside the microwave. The signals captured on a music recording or videotape are the software that tell a CD player or the VCR what electrical pulses to send to the speakers or to your television set to recreate the sounds of Mahler's Tenth Symphony or the sights of *Terminator 2*.

In personal computer systems, just about anything you can see, hold, feel, or taste (if you're so inclined) is hardware—microchips, monitor, keyboard, printer, modem. Software is intangible. You can hold the medium on which computer software is recorded—a floppy disk or hard drive—but the software itself is an abstract collection of instructions that results in your hardware performing specific, nonabstract tasks.

For software to work properly, it must be designed for specific hardware. If you were to transfer the recorded signals from a videotape to an audiotape, those signals would produce only meaningless noise when read by an audiotape player. Similarly, a program written for an IBM-compatible PC would generate only nonsense—if you could get it to do anything at all—on a Macintosh computer.

Between hardware and most other software is the *operating system*. The operating system is actually another software program, but of a special type. It doesn't let you write letters, calculate budgets, or track an inventory, but it lets programs that do all those things—called *application software*—work with the hardware.

It's possible to write software that doesn't need an operating system; such software sends instructions directly to the microprocessor and other hardware components of the PC. But an operating system performs two tasks—making things easier for programmers and making sure programs run on all similar classes of PCs. These tasks are so important that, for the most part, programmers don't try to write application software that speaks directly to hardware. The operating system relieves programmers of much of the drudgery of handling common operations. Without an operating system, each programmer would have to invent from scratch a way for a program to display text or graphics on screen, a way for it to send data to the printer, a way for it to read or write disk files, and a multitude of other functions that mesh software with hardware.

An operating system, however, does more than make life easier for programmers. It also assures that a program works the same way on different PCs. It disguises any differences between the hardware in one brand of computer and hardware in another brand, so that the same application will work on both.

In this part of *How Software Works*, we'll actually spend little time on application software. Instead, we'll look at the microprocessor and the operating system. The way they work is fundamental to how application programs work—these elements affect not only the mechanics of your PC system, but also the look and feel of software applications and the power and speed with which they operate.

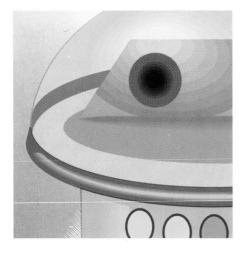

How the Microprocessor Runs Software

A PERSONAL COMPUTER'S microprocessor is a complex collection of thousands or even millions of microscopic on/off switches called *transistors*. The transistors are laid out in a microchip along circuits made up of superfine traces of aluminum. When the transistors are arranged in certain patterns, parts of the microprocessors are designated to hold data and others become capable of manipulating that data in various ways.

The on/off states of the transistors lend themselves handily to representing *binary numbers*, the form in which data and software code are stored. In the binary system, there are only two digits, 0 and 1, and these represent all numbers. The decimal number 1 is also 1 in binary, but 2 is 10, 3 is 11, 4 is 100, 5 is 101, 6 is 110, 7 is 111, and so on. A transistor that's turned off represents a 0; a transistor that's turned on stands for a 1. Each single 0 or 1 is called a *bit*. Eight bits make up a *byte,* and 1,024 bytes make up a *kilobyte* (K).

A computer sees both software code and data as a series of binary numbers. If you could shrink yourself to the size of a bacterium, go inside a chip, and see how the transistors in the microchips that make up a PC's *random-access memory* (RAM) are switched—on or off—you'd find a vast panorama of 0s and 1s, but you'd have no way to determine which portions of that array represent code and which represent data.

Intel's 80386, 80486, and Pentium microprocessors, along with their imitators, are 32-bit processors, which means that they can manipulate binary numbers that contain up to 32 bits. The largest 32-bit binary number is 11111111111111111111111111111111, which translates to the decimal number 4,294,967,295. Performing arithmetic on any number larger than that requires breaking the number into smaller components, performing the mathematical operations on the parts, and then combining the results.

The number 4,294,967,295 is significant in another way. All memory is identified with an *address;* 4,294,967,295 represents the upper limit to the amount of memory that the processor can address. Each byte of data in a PC's memory chips is numbered to create a *physical,* or *real,* address that represents the location of the actual transistors making up that byte in RAM or ROM chips. Because software applications can't know the physical addresses on the memory on every PC, a different addressing scheme—called a *logical address*—is used by the software. The microprocessor, in combination with the PC's operating system, uses logical addresses, which are symbolic rather than physical, and translates those logical addresses into physical addresses when reading and writing data.

Despite the ability of modern processors to address more than 4 million kilobytes of RAM, most PCs depend on operating-system tricks when they must use more than 640 kilobytes. The processor used in the first IBM PC—an Intel 8088—is a 16-bit processor, which means that it can manipulate a maximum of 16 bits of data. That means the largest address of a memory location can be only 1111111111111111 (16 bits filled with the value 1), which allows only 64 kilobytes of RAM to be used directly by the 8088.

To make more RAM usable, the creators of MS-DOS—the operating system that was designed to work with the 8088—devised a *segmented memory scheme* that combines two 16-bit binary numbers in a way that creates a 20-bit address. With this method, DOS can use the 8088 to address up to 1,024 kilobytes, or 1 *megabyte* (MB), of RAM. (Of that 1 megabyte, however, only 640 kilobytes is used by DOS for running programs. The rest of the megabyte of memory is left for various hardware devices that require memory addresses.)

The 80286, the processor that followed the 8088, can directly address up to 16 megabytes of RAM, but is hindered by the DOS limitation on the amount of RAM that can be addressed. The Intel 80386 and newer processors can use even more memory, but face the same limitation when used in *real mode,* a way of operating developed to mimic how an 8088 chip works. (The 80386, 80486, and Pentium chips also have a *protected mode* that takes full advantage of their capacities to address memory directly and to use special instructions. Protected mode requires OS/2, Windows NT, or some other advanced operating system.) In real mode, special programs called *memory managers* act as an extension to DOS, allowing the processors to use megabytes of RAM while continuing to use the DOS segmented memory scheme.

Newer operating systems, such as OS/2 and Windows NT, use a *flat memory scheme* that allows them to address directly the full range of memory that 32-bit processors are capable of using.

In this chapter, we'll look at how a segmented memory scheme works and how an 80386 microprocessor uses software code and data stored in memory. An Intel 80386 microprocessor is used here as an example because it represents a significant departure from earlier processors in the ways memory may be addressed and in its built-in instruction sets. Earlier processors do not have all the special function components found in the 80386. The newer 80486 and Pentium microprocessors are similar in concept to the 80386, but have other specialized components designed to handle floating-point numerical calculations and to speed the passage of code and data through the chip.

How DOS Uses Segmented Memory

1 To access a physical memory location, DOS first loads a 16-bit address segment into one of the microprocessor's *registers*, which are specific transistor locations within the processor, used to hold data while the data is manipulated by the processor.

0 0 0 1 0 0 1 0 0 0

2 The processor shifts the 16-bit address four places to the left. This is the same as multiplying the number by 16 or adding four zeros to it to create a 20-bit binary number. But with those four extra zeros, the 20-bit numbers can represent only 1 out of every 16 memory locations—the one whose 20-bit address ends in four zeros. This is a *segment address*.

0 0 0 1 0 0 1 0 0 0 0 1 1 0 1

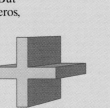

0 1 0 1 0 1 1 0 0 1

0 0 0 1 0 1 1 1 1 0 0 1 1 0

3 The processor adds a second 16-bit number that is the *relative address*, or the *offset*, from the segment address. The result is a complete 20-bit number that represents a *linear address*.

NOTE OS/2 and Windows NT use a flat memory scheme, which addresses up to 4 gigabytes (G) of RAM directly without having to go through the address manipulations DOS uses.

4 The processor locates the memory address by first finding the segment address and then the relative address offset from that segment address.

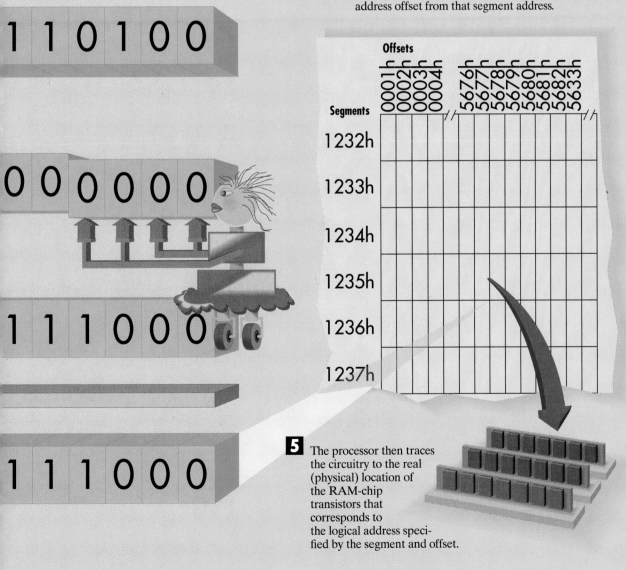

5 The processor then traces the circuitry to the real (physical) location of the RAM-chip transistors that corresponds to the logical address specified by the segment and offset.

How an 80386 Microprocessor Runs Software

3 Data or code is retrieved from RAM by the *bus interface unit* (BIU), which converts segments and offsets of addresses to a linear address. All code or data must also pass from the microprocessor through the BIU to reach RAM.

BUS INTERFACE UNIT

2 The microprocessor begins reading in the program's code, starting at the program's first byte in RAM. It reads each consecutive byte and executes the instructions contained in that code. This continues until one of two things happens: The microprocessor encounters an instruction that orders it to jump, loop, or otherwise move to a different location in the program; or an *interrupt* signal is generated by software or a hardware device, such as a keyboard, that demands the processor's immediate attention.

1 When you run a program, your PC's operating system copies the program from the hard drive, where the program is stored permanently, to RAM.

9 Through a process called *pipelining,* all the operations performed by the various units may be occurring simultaneously. The objective of pipelining is to ensure that components of the processor spend as little time as possible idling while waiting for further data or instructions.

PAGING UNIT

PROCE

8 The *paging unit* performs the last step in converting the logical address to a physical address by making any adjustments that may be necessary when the processor is using sections of memory called *pages*. The unit generates the actual signals that will be placed on the pins of the processor's address bus. The paging unit passes the address to the BIU, which uses the address to send data resulting from the code execution to the correct location in physical memory.

4 When the BIU is not busy with operations that involve the execution of instructions, the *code prefetch unit* asks the BIU to send it the next instructions waiting for execution. The code is thus separated from data and placed in the prefetch unit's own 16-byte queue, where it can be retrieved quickly by the instruction decode unit.

DATA

CODE

PREFETCH UNIT

INSTRUCTION DECODE UNIT

5 The *instruction decode unit* reads instruction bytes from the prefetch queue, translates them to the simpler instructions and control signals used by the processor, and holds the translations in its own queue until they are requested by the execution unit.

REGISTERS

EXECUTION UNIT

6 The *execution unit* retrieves instructions waiting in the instruction decode unit's queue and executes them. Generally, the execution takes place in the *data unit,* which contains eight 32-bit registers that are the execution unit's scratch pad—a place to hold the data being manipulated and the results of those manipulations. Most of those manipulations are performed by the *arithmetic logic unit* (ALU). The execution unit also contains two other subdivisions. The *control unit* contains specialized microcode that speeds up multiplication, division, and addressing calculations. If the CPU is working in protected mode, the *protection test unit* monitors memory accesses to detect requests that violate the segmented memory scheme.

SEGMENTATION UNIT

SSOR

7 The *segmentation unit* performs the first step in converting a 20-bit logical memory address into a physical address by breaking the 20-bit number into its component segment and offset.

C H A P T E R

How the BIOS Works with Software

MAGINE IF YOU sat down in the driver's seat of a car only to discover that there were no steering wheel—it had been replaced by an airplane joystick. What's more, instead of a brake pedal, say you were confronted with a button that you had to operate with your nose.

Luckily, you don't ever have to face that problem. Car mechanisms may differ—some have power steering, front-wheel drive, and disk brakes, while others don't—but you don't need to know how these mechanisms work. You only need to know how to turn the steering wheel and press the brake pedal. The intervening layer—the levers, gears and hydraulic systems—separates you from the mechanisms that do the real work. These mechanisms translate your actions into car movements: a change of direction or slowing down.

In the same way, your personal computer, too, has a layer that separates you and your application software from the down-and-dirty workings of your hardware. In fact, there are two layers; you encounter the first whenever you do something at the C: prompt. This layer is called the operating system, and we'll look at it in the next chapter. But there's a layer even more fundamental that lies between the operating system and the hardware—the *BIOS,* or *basic input/output system.*

The BIOS lets your applications and various operating systems work in just one way, regardless of the type of IBM-compatible computer they're running on. It translates the commands from software into the signals that a particular PC needs to carry out those commands. Because those hardware-level signals may differ from one PC to another, the BIOS is crucial for making sure that software works the same no matter what brand or model of IBM-compatible PC it's running on.

Without the BIOS, programmers would have to rewrite operating systems and application software for each hardware configuration. The operating system would have to know the exact signals needed to read and write files, recognize keystrokes, and display text for each of the specific drives, keyboards, and monitors used in thousands of combinations of components. Buy a new, bigger hard disk and you'd have to get a new version of your word processor just to save documents to it.

The BIOS handles the nitty-gritty of sending and recognizing the correct electrical signals associated with various hardware components. Instead of having to know how a certain drive works, an application program needs to know only how to communicate through the operating system to the

BIOS. The BIOS takes care of the task requested by an application. It's like having a highly efficient assistant who knows how the office filing system works. All you have to do is leave a file in the out basket, and the assistant makes sure it gets into the right drawer in the right cabinet.

The working part of the BIOS is the code located in one or more read-only memory (ROM) chips—a type of memory that cannot be modified. These chips normally are located on your PC's main circuit board, or motherboard, where they're installed at the factory. It's one part of your PC that, ordinarily, you don't replace.

PC manufacturers who want to create an IBM-compatible personal computer are most concerned with the BIOS. The code in the BIOS of a PC clone is what determines how compatible it is with an IBM personal computer. When the original IBM PC was introduced, most of its components—such as the microprocessor and the floppy drives—were off-the-shelf devices that anyone wanting to clone an IBM could use. What made the IBM PC distinctive was the code in its BIOS chips. Other companies wanting to produce PCs that could run the same software as the IBM PC ran had to duplicate the functionality of the IBM BIOS (without copying the code directly, which is illegal).

In those early days of personal computers, some manufacturers either failed to reproduce all the functionality of the IBM BIOS or else they made so-called improvements to some functions so they would, say, execute faster. At the same time, some software authors were developing their own shortcuts by going around the operating system—the approved way for applications to communicate with the BIOS—and sending instructions directly to specific memory locations in the BIOS. The results were unpredictable and usually disastrous. In the first couple of years of the PC boom, it was a crapshoot to work with any PC except those made by companies that were scrupulous about creating their BIOS, such as Compaq. Today that is rarely a problem.

In addition to the system BIOS that comes with your personal computer, other components—such as video adapters and disk-drive controllers—are likely to have their own BIOS chips. In fact, the memory scheme of MS-DOS reserves specific memory addresses above 640 kilobytes for video BIOS code. The code in these BIOS chips is loaded when you turn on your PC. Sometimes a *device driver*—an extension to the basic operating system—must be loaded through a line in a file named CONFIG.SYS to make the computer aware of these extra BIOS codes.

Except for a fleeting message that appears on screen as you boot your computer and it loads the BIOS code, you will rarely be aware of your PC's BIOS codes and what they're doing. Which is exactly the way it should be. A good BIOS is a silent but vital partner.

How the BIOS Works with Software

1 When you choose the commands for saving a file in your word processor, the word processor sends the command and the data to be saved to the operating system. (In a Windows environment, Windows acts as an extension of the operating system to help handle common operations.)

4 The BIOS instructions are translated into the electrical signals needed to move the drive's read/write heads to the proper locations on the disk and to create the magnetic signals that record the data on the disk's surface.

2 The operating environment checks to make sure that there are no problems with the command to save the data. For example, it makes sure that the file name is a legal one, and that you're not trying to save over a file that's marked read-only. If everything is OK, the operating environment turns the job of writing the data to disk over to the BIOS.

WORD PROC
FILE
SAVE

OPERATING SYSTEM

PROCESSOR

RAM

BIOS

INPUT

OUTPUT

BIOS

3 The BIOS sends the data to the disk-drive controller along with a prepackaged routine of commands tailored specifically to that controller or drive. (The commands may exist as part of the code in a BIOS chip on the controller or on the disk drive's circuitry.)

CHAPTER 3

How the Operating System Interacts with the BIOS

THERE ARE TWO types of software. Application software—word processors, database managers, electronic spreadsheets, and desktop publishing—lets you accomplish the work that you bought a personal computer for in the first place. System software—the operating systems, memory managers, disk and printing caches, and so forth—controls how your application software runs.

Of all the system software, the most important is the operating system. An operating system is the software equivalent of the BIOS (basic input/output system) code contained in ROM chips. It works as another intermediary between your application programs and your hardware. Just as the BIOS defines how the hardware works, the operating system defines how your software works by establishing a set of rules all software must follow—for example, how many and what kind of characters may be included in a file's name. The operating system also includes a set of operations—such as reading and writing disk files—which applications can use.

The application software that follows these rules needn't be concerned with the details of how files are laid out in tracks and sectors on the disk. The application merely has to issue a command to the operating system to save a file—conforming to the rule for file names—and the operating system then communicates with the BIOS to transfer the file from RAM to disk. The name of the most commonly used operating system, MS-DOS, derives from the name of its manufacturer, Microsoft, and from the term *disk operating system,* which describes what its creators considered to be its most crucial function.

But defining disk operations is not the only function of an operating system. Another important task is deciding how memory is used. In its basic configuration, MS-DOS is not equipped to handle more than 1 megabyte of RAM. Although today that seems a ludicrously small amount, at the time DOS was created, personal computers could handle (at most) 64 kilobytes of RAM, and 1 megabyte was considered an unnecessarily large capacity. Newer operating systems, such as OS/2 and Windows NT, were designed from the outset to work with newer, more powerful processors and don't have the same memory limitations as MS-DOS. (Both OS/2 and Windows NT are superior to MS-DOS. They both provide better protection against crashes, smoother multitasking, and direct access to more memory. But this book uses DOS for its examples because DOS is the most prevalent operating system. Note that Windows—plain Windows, not Windows NT—is not a true operating system because it requires DOS. The non-NT version of Windows cannot run on a PC by itself. Windows, however elaborate it may be, is just another addition—like a device driver or a utilities program—that extends the abilities of DOS.)

OS/2 and Windows NT remind us also of how much an operating system is responsible for the look and feel of its application software. The MS-DOS interface was designed for hardware for which memory was at a premium; as a consequence, DOS was made as efficient as possible in its use of memory. This resulted in a display based on text—which can be displayed on a computer screen through the use of some simple, economical shorthand codes—and a few simple graphical elements. Windows NT and OS/2, on the other hand, draw lines, boxes, arrows, and other graphical elements that you use to control operations. The graphics require that there be enough memory and computation power to control every area of the screen at all times.

Under DOS, the main method by which a PC user communicates with the software and operating system is also based on text. The user types command words or makes selections from text menus. Graphic operating systems display text and menus, but they are object oriented instead of text oriented. *Object oriented* means that the objects displayed on the screen—such as buttons, boxes, or lists—mean something to the operating system, just as words mean something to DOS. Using a mouse to point at and click on an on-screen object in a graphic interface is equivalent to typing a word at a command prompt.

An operating system is not a simple piece of software; it is made up of a collection of utilities and *device drivers*—programs that control hardware devices, such as mice, drives, and display adapters. Device drivers are necessary because a PC's BIOSs cannot possibly be large enough or current enough to contain the microcode needed to control every conceivable hardware device. Instead, the operating system uses the code contained in files called device drivers to operate certain devices. Some of these device drivers are loaded into memory through the CONFIG.SYS file; others are loaded from disk whenever they are needed. They act like extensions of the operating system, translating the operations instigated in software into the signals needed to control hard drives, printers, tape backups, optical drives, or memory.

In this chapter, we'll look at how DOS uses memory to hold different parts of the operating system, the BIOS, and the applications. We'll also examine *interrupts*, which are used by hardware devices and by software to get the attention of the operating system.

How the Operating System Uses Memory

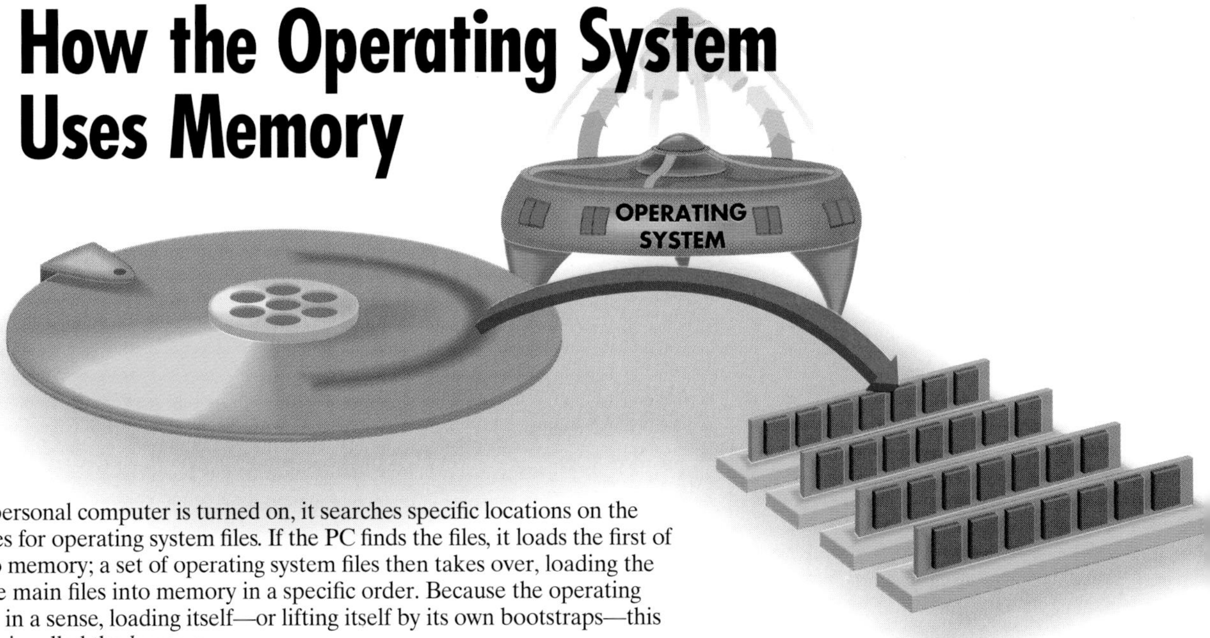

OPERATING SYSTEM

1 When a personal computer is turned on, it searches specific locations on the disk drives for operating system files. If the PC finds the files, it loads the first of them into memory; a set of operating system files then takes over, loading the rest of the main files into memory in a specific order. Because the operating system is, in a sense, loading itself—or lifting itself by its own bootstraps—this operation is called the *boot-up*.

2 At the lowest part of memory, the operating system loads a table of interrupt vectors. When the operating system receives special codes called interrupts, it uses the table to determine where in memory it can find matching instructions. DOS also uses a small area just above the interrupt table to hold the BIOS data called *flags* that record the state of various system conditions. The same area also acts as a buffer to store keystrokes that come in faster than the system can process them.

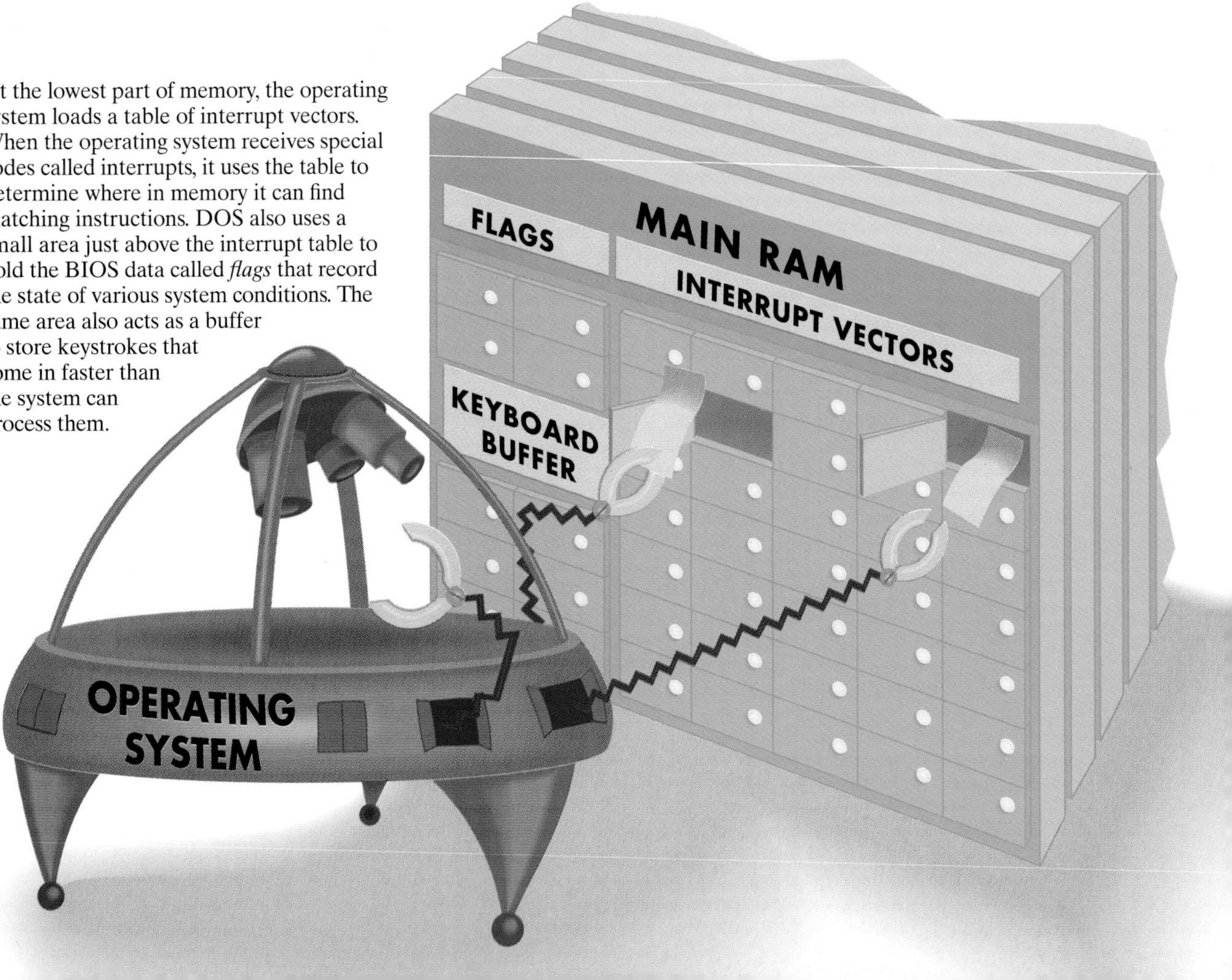

FLAGS

MAIN RAM

INTERRUPT VECTORS

KEYBOARD BUFFER

OPERATING SYSTEM

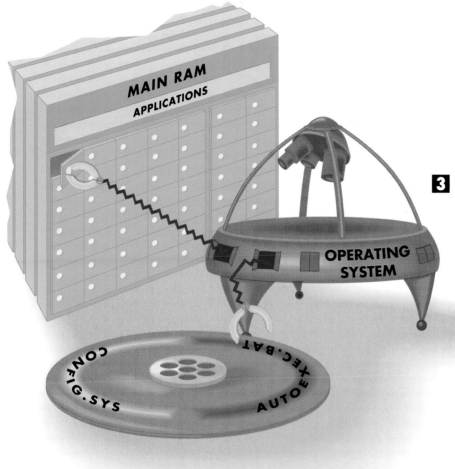

3 A large expanse of memory just above the BIOS flags and keyboard buffer is used for device drivers, utility programs, and application programs. When DOS reads the CONFIG.SYS and AUTOEXEC.BAT files, it looks for command lines to load drivers or *memory-resident* programs; when it finds such a command line, DOS normally puts the driver or program at the start of this large memory area. (Memory-resident programs are those that continue to be active even when application programs are running.) Device drivers usually remain loaded until the PC is turned off. Memory-resident programs can be unloaded if no other programs are loaded after them.

4 Application programs are loaded in RAM beginning in the area just above the drivers and memory-resident programs. Because of the way DOS is designed, applications cannot extend beyond the 640K address of RAM. [*Continued on next page.*]

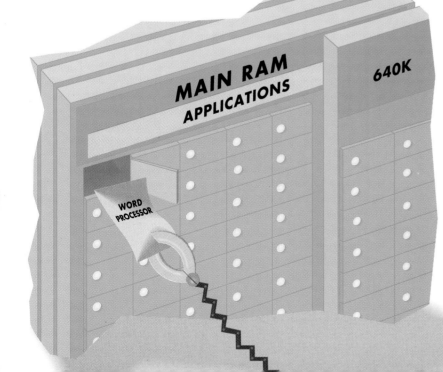

How the Operating System Uses Memory

5 A small area of memory just before the 640K barrier is used to hold COMMAND.COM, a DOS program that includes built-in commands such as DIR, COPY, and DELETE. This area can be overwritten by a large application, in which case DOS will reload COMMAND.COM from disk when the user exits the application.

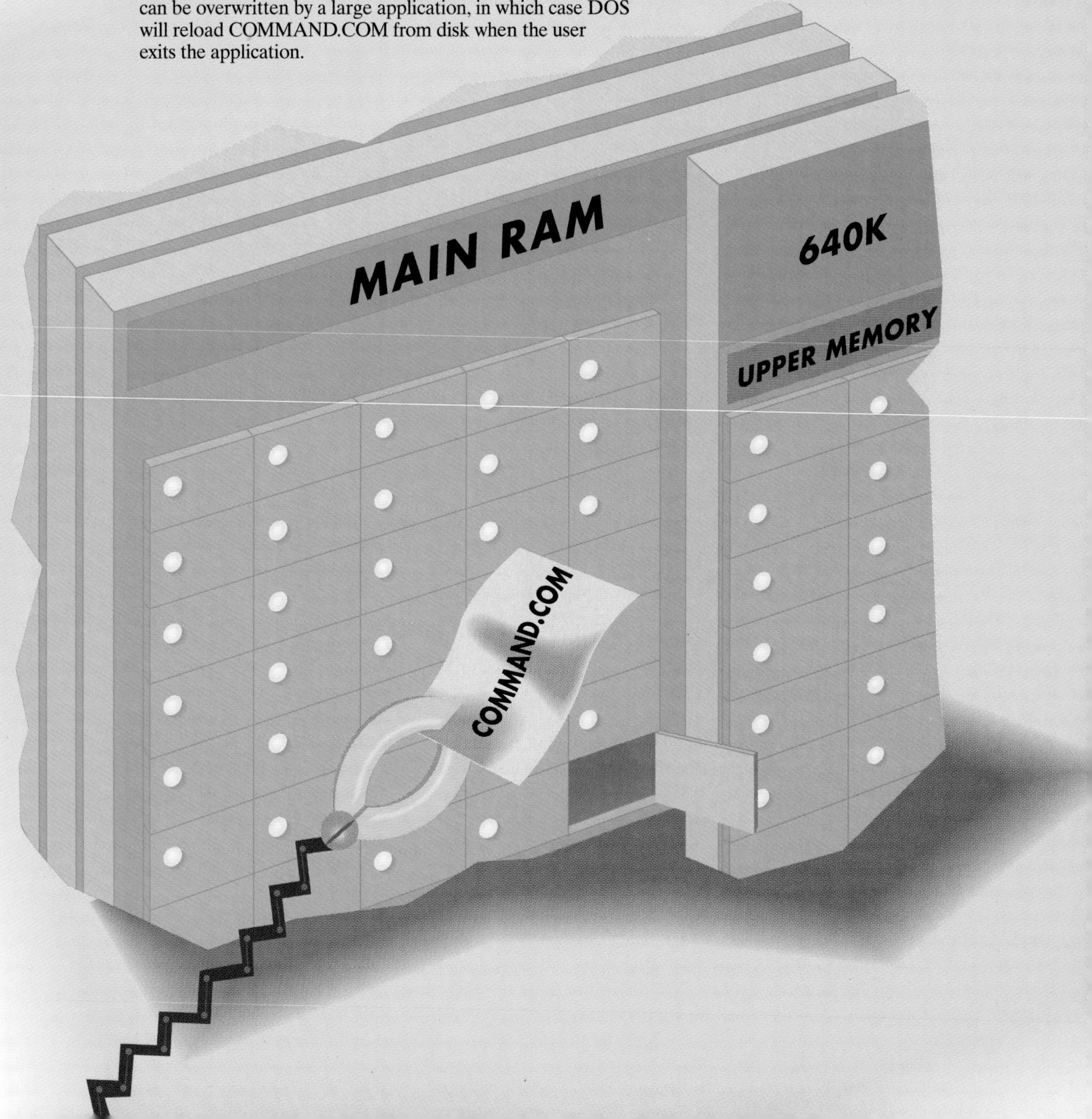

MAIN RAM

640K

UPPER MEMORY

COMMAND.COM

6 The range of memory between 640K and 1MB—called *upper memory*—is not ordinarily used for application programs, but instead holds various BIOSs for such hardware as display adapters, disk controllers, and network cards. The last 64K of high RAM is used for the main BIOS code. *Memory managers*—such as HIMEM.SYS, which is supplied with DOS—can relocate device drivers and memory-resident programs into high RAM.

How Interrupts Work

INTERRUPT

1 Various hardware events—such as a keystroke, data coming through a serial or parallel port, or some software events that need an immediate response from the processor—generate a special type of signal called an *interrupt*. As its name implies, an interrupt causes the PC to temporarily stop what it is doing to divert its attention to the service required by the signal. In this example, the interrupt is caused by the user pressing a key.

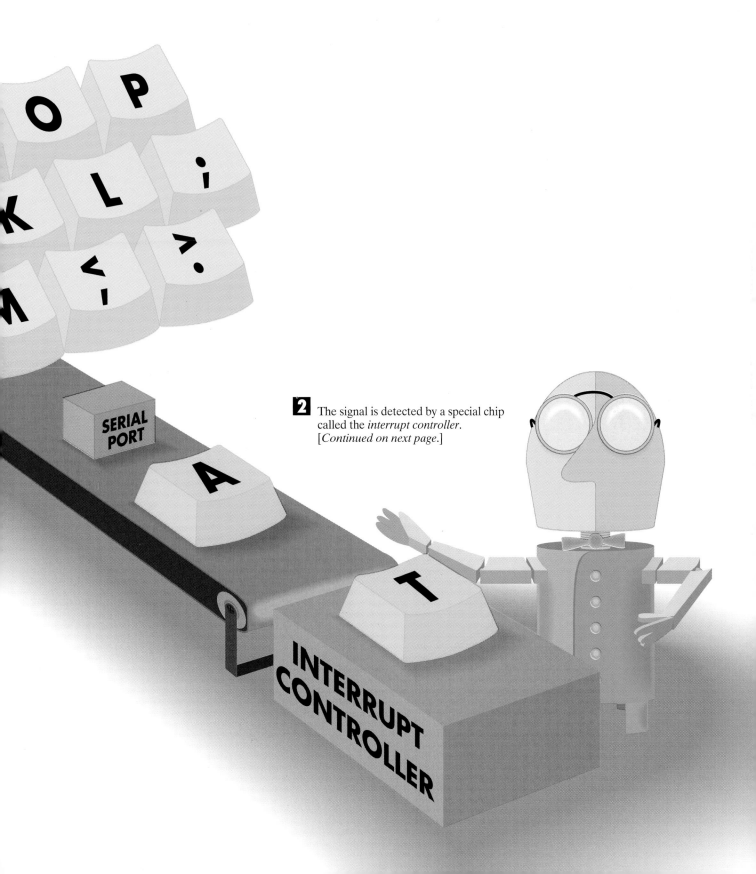

2 The signal is detected by a special chip called the *interrupt controller*. [*Continued on next page*.]

How Interrupts Work

3 The interrupt controller notifies the PC's microprocessor that an interrupt has occurred and demands the processor's immediate attention.

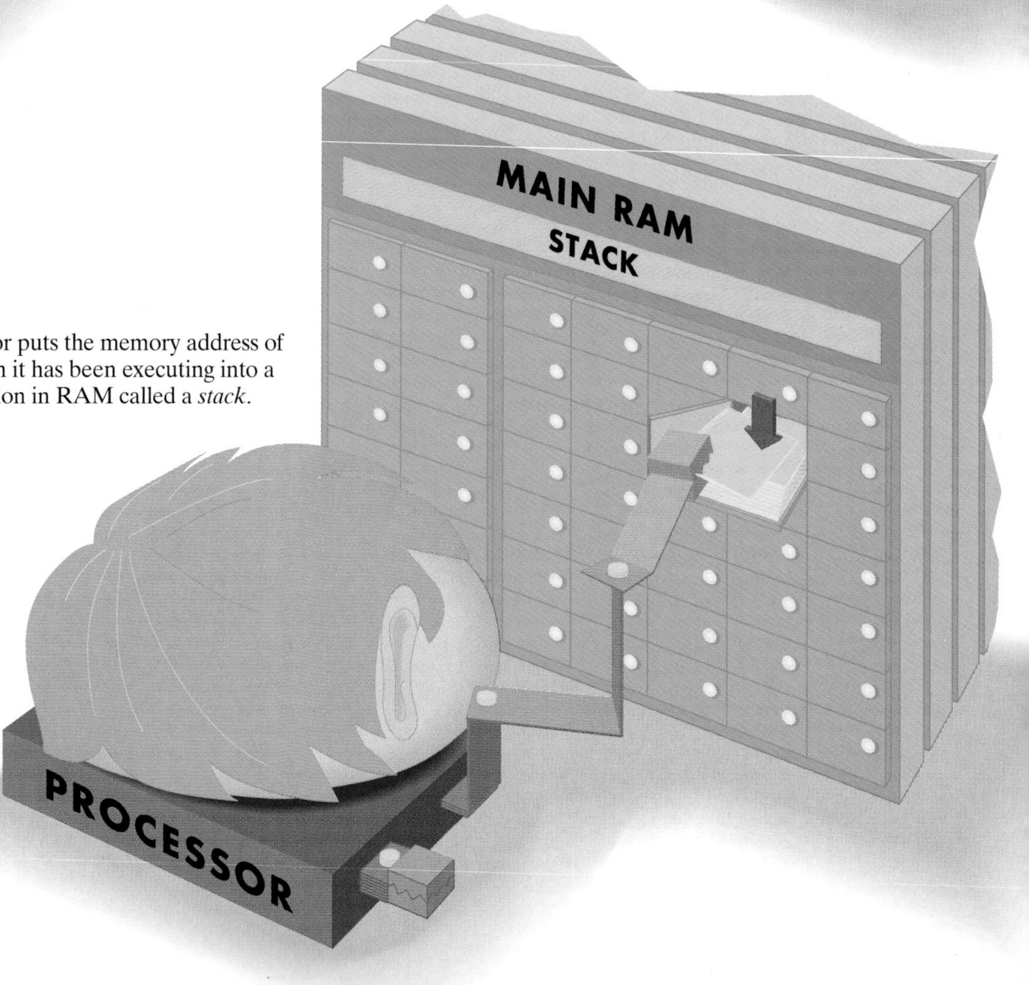

INTERRUPT CONTROLLER

PROCESSOR

MAIN RAM
STACK

4 The processor puts the memory address of the operation it has been executing into a special location in RAM called a *stack*.

PROCESSOR

5 The processor retrieves the number of the interrupt from the interrupt controller. Each interrupt is associated with a particular number and, in some cases, a second number denoting a particular *service*—a specific hardware function that is being requested by the interrupt.

6 The processor inspects the interrupt table that was loaded into RAM when the operating system was loaded. Listed under the interrupt number, the processor finds a specific memory address. [*Continued on next page.*]

How Interrupts Work

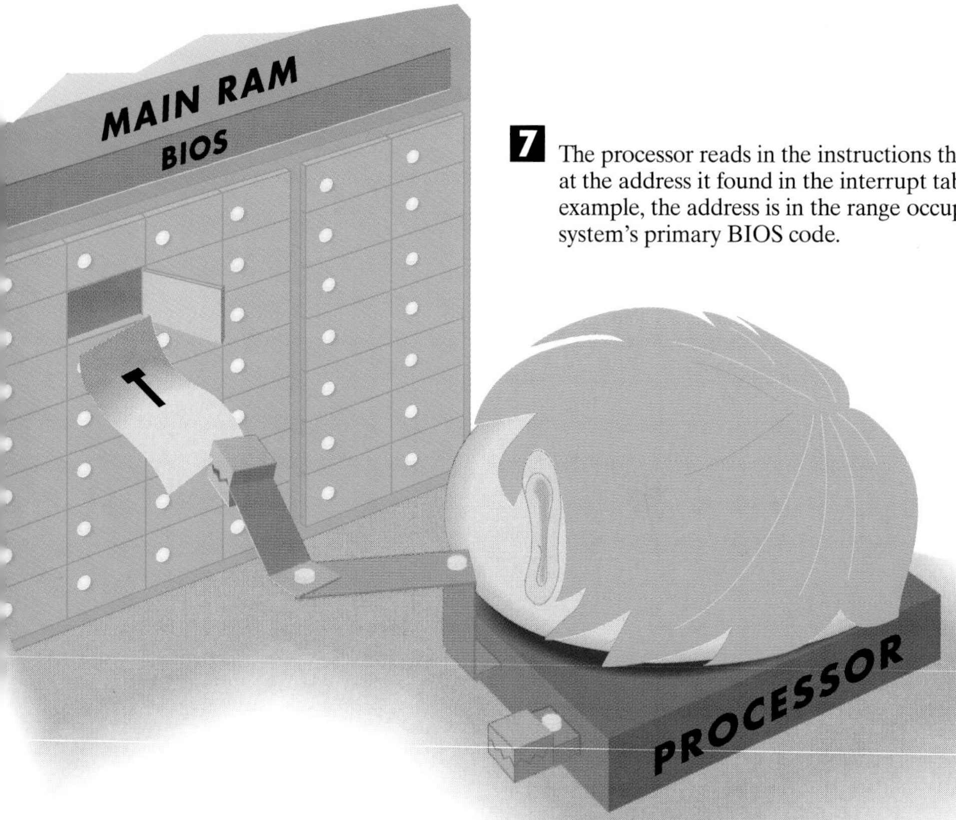

7 The processor reads in the instructions that begin at the address it found in the interrupt table. In this example, the address is in the range occupied by the system's primary BIOS code.

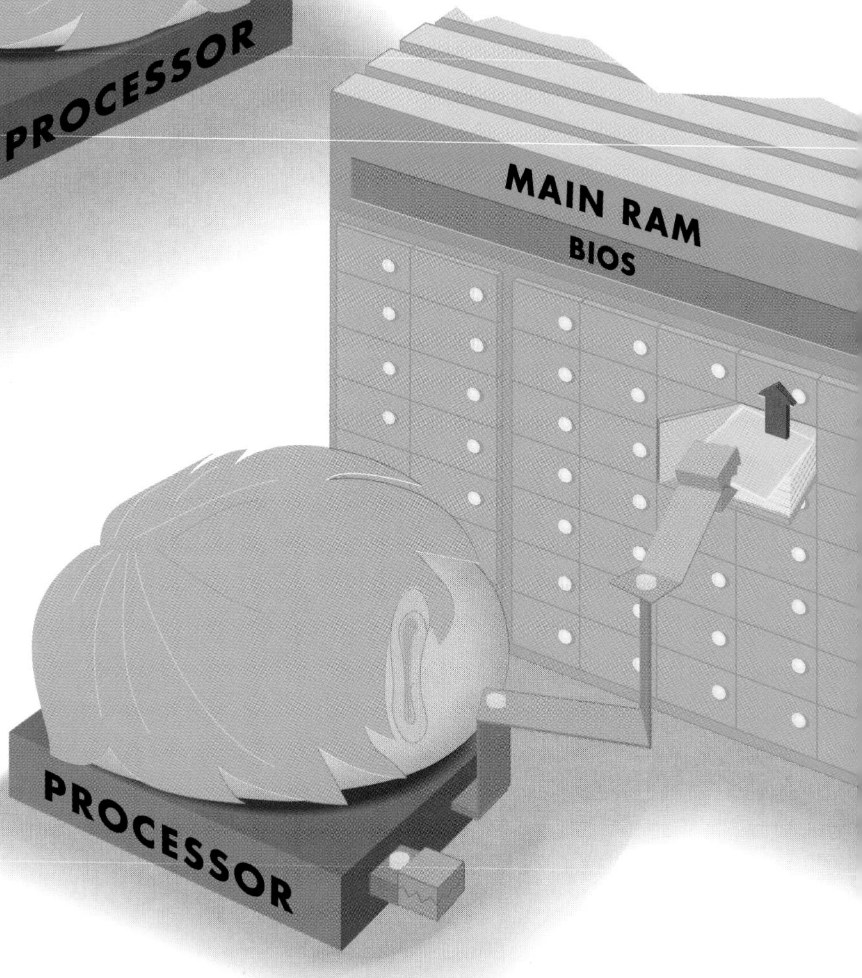

MAIN RAM

BIOS

PROCESSOR

MAIN RAM

BIOS

PROCESSOR

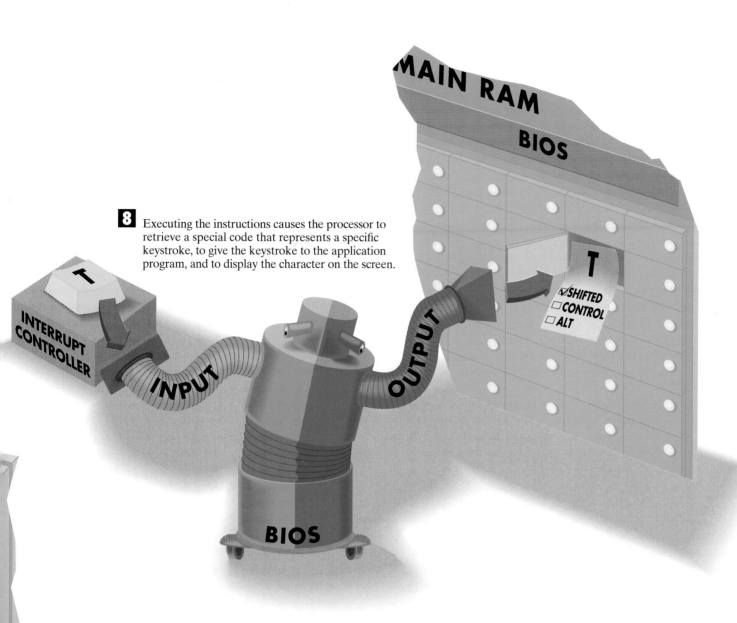

8 Executing the instructions causes the processor to retrieve a special code that represents a specific keystroke, to give the keystroke to the application program, and to display the character on the screen.

9 When the instructions found in the interrupt address are completed, the processor retrieves the address it had placed on the stack and continues to execute those instructions where it left off.

CHAPTER

How Memory Managers Work

ORIGINALLY, MS-DOS was not intended to manage more than 1 megabyte of memory, of which only 640 kilobytes were designated for the operating system and applications. Even when microprocessors were developed to handle more memory, programmers and users were still stuck with the same restraints—until programmers developed ingenious devices that gave PCs running DOS access to more than 1 megabyte of RAM, in turn giving applications more elbow room in the 640 kilobytes allotted to them. Those devices are called *memory managers.*

Later versions of DOS provide their own memory managers in the form of files called HIMEM.SYS and EMM386.EXE. Other, more vigorous memory managers are found in products such as QEMM-386 and 386MAX. These are created by developers other than Microsoft, the company that sells MS-DOS. In essence, all memory managers function in the same way, although QEMM-386 and 386MAX are generally more versatile.

Whatever their origins, all memory managers perform the same two basic tasks: finding spare nooks and crannies of *upper memory*—the area between 640 kilobytes and 1 megabyte—where they can load device drivers and memory-resident programs (all of which otherwise would take up valuable space below the 640 kilobytes barrier), and giving programs access to memory above 1 megabyte. This memory can take three forms. One is a special location just above 1 megabyte called the *high memory area* (HMA). The second is *expanded memory*, also called EMS (for *expanded memory specification*), an early effort to overcome the limitations of DOS by giving programs access to more memory. The third type of memory that a memory manager handles is *extended memory,* also called XMS (*extended memory specification*). (Because the terms *expanded memory* and *extended memory* are so similar, it helps to have some way to remember which is which. Try this: Ex**P**anded memory will work on an original **P**C; ex**T**ended memory will work only on an A**T**-class or later computer.

EMS is decreasing in importance because it is slow and provides more memory only for data used by a program, not for the program code itself. EMS is limited primarily to DOS applications. Expanded memory can be used on any PC, including those with the original Intel 8088 processor; because 8088 processors are used so little today, however, expanded memory is no longer a significant advantage.

Unlike EMS, extended memory can be used only on a PC that's AT-class or newer. Like EMS, extended RAM can be used for data. But it can also be used for program code, provided the program has been written using a type of code called a *DOS extender*. DOS extenders, in turn, generally require an Intel 80386 (or newer) processor. There have been few major applications written using DOS extenders, but there is one significant environment using the extenders to access extended RAM: Windows.

Windows is capable of running several applications simultaneously because it can load them into extended memory and use special features of the 80386, 80486, and Pentium processors. Windows, in combination with a DOS memory manager, becomes the liaison between the applications and DOS whenever any of the applications need one of the services provided in conventional memory (memory below 1 megabyte).

Memory managers will become less important as newer operating systems, such as OS/2 and Windows NT, become more prevalent. OS/2 and Windows NT are written to use the memory management and protection abilities that are built into the Intel 80386 processor and its descendants, and so have no need of a separate software memory manager. These newer operating systems can provide gigabytes of memory to all programs designed to work with them.

But for some time to come, a memory manager will be part of the standard ammunition of PC users who want to get the most out of today's memory-hungry programs.

How a Memory Manager Uses Expanded and Extended RAM

1 When a PC is turned on and a memory manager is loaded, the memory manager sets up a device driver that changes the interrupt vectors for any DOS operations that attempt to access memory.

2 If the line **DOS=HIGH** is included in the CONFIG.SYS file, when the computer boots, the memory manager loads parts of the DOS system files—IO.SYS, MSDOS.SYS, and COMMAND.COM—into a special portion of memory called the *high memory area* (HMA), located just past the 1MB address. This frees about 42K in conventional memory that can then be used by application programs.

3 If a PC's memory management is configured to handle expanded memory as well as extended memory, the memory manager also sets aside a *page frame*—a 64K section of the upper memory that exists between 640K and 1MB. The frame will be used as a gateway through which programs are given access to extended RAM that the memory manager allows programs to treat as expanded RAM.

4 The memory manager inspects upper memory to determine what addresses in that area are not being used by BIOS code for a device (such as a video adapter, drive controller, or network card). The manager assigns any unused addresses to extended RAM, creating what are called *upper memory blocks* (UMBs). [*Continued on next page.*]

How a Memory Manager Uses Expanded and Extended RAM

5 When a device driver or memory-resident program is loaded through a memory manager—this is done with a command such as **LOADHIGH C:\DOS\DOSKEY**—the manager inspects the UMBs to determine if one of them is large enough to hold the driver or program. If the manager finds one large enough, it loads the driver or program into the address of the UMB and sets a pointer so that any program wanting to use the driver or the memory-resident program will know where to find it.

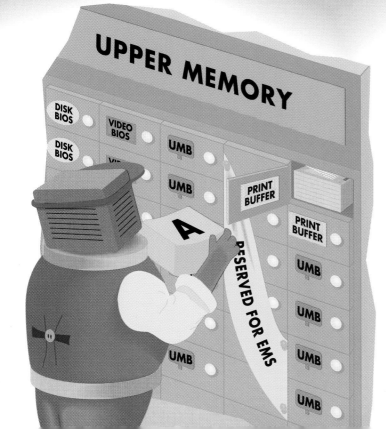

6 After a memory manager has established a map of memory and the links among various portions of the map, an interrupt from either hardware or a program is routed first through the memory manager's own device driver to determine if the interrupt is requesting an operation that involves access to extended RAM, expanded RAM, or UMBs.

7 If an interrupt requests a function loaded in a UMB, the memory manager points the interrupt to the correct UMB address, which contains extended memory that operates as conventional RAM. [*Continued on next page.*]

How a Memory Manager Uses Expanded and Extended RAM

8 If a program requires expanded memory, the memory manager puts into the page frame four 16K pages of extended RAM, which the program uses as if they were expanded RAM. As different requests for expanded memory occur, the memory manager changes the addresses of expanded memory represented by the four pages in the frame. By juggling these addresses, the memory manager can provide access to megabytes of expanded RAM, one 16K page at a time.

If a program requires extended RAM, it accesses a function of the CPU called *protected mode*. Normally, under DOS, the CPU works in *real mode*. In real mode, an 80286, 80386, 80486, or Pentium CPU operates as if it were an 8086 processor. In protected mode, the CPU addresses memory differently so that it can access up to 4 gigabytes of memory and run several real-mode sessions simultaneously. Any application running in any of the real-mode sessions acts as if it were the only program using the PC. If any of the sessions attempt to request a service from part of the hardware that may be in use by another session—such as the hard drive—the CPU's protected mode intercepts the requests and referees them so the sessions are not sending conflicting hardware requests at the same time.

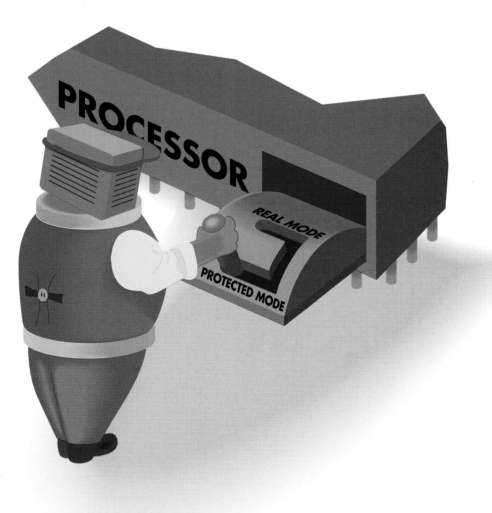

HOW PROGRAMMING LANGUAGES WORK

CONTENTS

YOUR MOST FUNDAMENTAL tool as an intelligent being is language. It is through language that you learn new information and share your knowledge, feelings, and experiences with others. Through language you can express any thought that has been expressed by any person throughout history, and you can capture scenes and events that came and went long before any camera could have recorded them. The world is controlled through language. Presidents to petty functionaries, generals to GIs, CEOs to clerks—all rely on language to give instructions to others and to provide the information needed to carry out those instructions.

For a computer, too, language is necessary if the machine is to function intelligently. Software is created with languages that provide instructions for telling the computer what to do and that define the data to which the instructions apply. Computer language is similar to human language in many ways. The nouns, verbs, prepositions, and objects found in English, for example, have their counterparts in computer languages. Software sentences have their own syntax, and the words that make up the languages have their own meanings.

Computer language is both more precise and more limited than English. An often-repeated story tells how, in an early attempt to use a computer to translate English into Russian, the phrase "The spirit is willing, but the flesh is weak" was interpreted as "The vodka is ready, but the meat is rotten." The story may well be apocryphal, but it illustrates a reality—that computers and their languages do not (as of now, at any rate) do a good job of managing the ambiguities and shades of meaning in human language that any four-year-old understands.

On the other hand, English cannot match the precision of computer language. Try, for example, to describe a simple spiral without using your hands. It's impossible in English. But because math is an integral part of computer languages, those languages can not only describe a spiral but can also provide the instructions to create an image of that spiral on a monitor or printer.

Just as there is more than one language for humans, so is there more than one computer language, even for the same type of computer. Generally, the various languages are described as being *low-level* or *high-level*. The more a computer language resembles ordinary English, the higher its level. On the lowest level is *machine language*; this is a series of codes, represented by numbers, that are used to communicate directly with the internal instructions of the PC's microprocessor. Deciphering machine language code or writing in it is as complex a task as one can tackle in computing. Luckily we don't have to do it. Programs called *interpreters* and *compilers* translate commands written in higher-level languages into machine language. We'll look at interpreters and compilers later in the book.

On a slightly higher level than machine language is *assembly language,* which uses simple words to supply step-by-step instructions for the computer to carry out. Assembly language directly manipulates the values contained in those parts of the microprocessor called *registers*. Where, for example, the hexadecimal code 40 is used in machine language to increase by one the value contained in register AX, assembly language uses the command INC AX to perform the same function. Although assembly language is more intelligible to humans than machine language codes are, assembly is still more difficult to use than are higher-level languages. Assembly remains popular among programmers, however, because it creates compact, fast code.

On the high end, languages such as C and Pascal allow programmers to write in words and terms that more closely parallel English. And the programmer using these languages need not be concerned with such minutiae as registers. Variations of the C language are the languages of choice today for most PC programming because C is powerful, reasonably simple to write and understand, and can easily be modified to allow a program written for one type of computer to be used on another.

Although most code can be written in C, often modern software consists of more than one program and is created with more than one language. Generally, software is a master program combined with a collection of subprograms, or *routines*, that are called on by the master program as needed. The master program is usually written in a high-level language, but routines may be written in other languages (frequently assembly) that are more suited to the tasks that the routines need to perform.

Whether high-level or low-level, all computer languages must provide similar abilities to the programs they are used to create. The exact words and syntax used for the commands may differ, but the languages must furnish a way to receive, or input, information from the keyboard, memory, ports, and files and a way to send, or output, information to the screen, memory, ports, and files. The languages must also provide internal logic. This logic takes the form of testing whether some condition is true or false and then performing an operation based on the results of that test. Languages must also have a way to hold and manipulate values; most often, these values are maintained in *variables*, so called because the values they contain can vary each time the program is run. Finally, languages have various ways of controlling the sequence of actions; usually depending on which conditions are encountered through logic tests, a program's operation may branch to another section of code, return to where it left off in an earlier section, or loop to repeat the same instructions until some logical condition is fulfilled. The types of input, output, logic, variables, and instruction flow are more complex and varied than this description indicates, and the precise words and syntax that represent the commands differ from language to language. But essentially any software you use, from the simplest utility to the most advanced spreadsheet, is a combination of these ingredients.

How Machine Language Works

NO MATTER WHAT software language a program has been written in, at the microprocessor level, the program is communicating its instructions to the processor in *machine language*. As the name implies, this language is the native tongue of the PC, which despite all the wonderful, intelligent things it can do, is still a machine.

Machine language takes the form of binary codes that tell the processor to *fetch* (read) and write data at specific locations in memory and to perform some mathematical or logical operation on the data. The processor performs these operations by manipulating values in special locations within the processor, called *registers*. Think of registers as scratch pads that the processor uses for all its temporary calculations, until it arrives at a final result. Registers may be used to facilitate arithmetic and logic operations or the transfer of data from one location in memory to another. Machine language codes tell the microprocessor what data to put into the registers and how to manipulate the data once it's there.

The number of registers and their sizes depend on the type of microprocessor. The Intel 8088, used in the original IBM PC, has four 16-bit registers for general-purpose use and four other registers—called *segment registers*—for tracking the addresses of code, data, stacks (temporary holding areas), and other information in memory. An Intel 80486 processor has eight 32-bit registers to use as scratchpads; six 16-bit registers for handling memory addressing; one 32-bit register that keeps track of various conditions, such as the sign of a number or whether interrupts are enabled; and another 32-bit register that maintains a pointer to the location of the next instruction to be executed. The larger and more plentiful registers are a superset of the 8088 registers—they can run anything that the earlier processor can run, and then some. The larger, more numerous registers are one feature that makes the 80486 so much more powerful than the 8088.

Machine language is often confused with *assembly language*. Working with the binary numbers that make up machine language is very difficult; instead of using machine code, assembly language uses mnemonic words, such as *mov* and *jmp*. The programmer writes in assembly, and the program is then translated to pure binary code.

The binary codes give instructions to the CPU and tell it which operands to use. *Operands* are the data that is manipulated by the instructions. The codes don't actually provide the operands; instead, they tell the CPU the addresses in memory where the operands can be found. The processor then copies the operands to the registers and carries out the instruction.

For all the seemingly intelligent tasks a personal computer can perform, essentially it's a simple-minded machine. The microprocessor that is the brains of a PC can perform only one simple instruction at a time. A group of these instructions, taken as a whole, results in a more complex task being performed.

For instance, for an older, less versatile processor, a software command to multiply 10×5 would be converted into a series of instructions to add 10 five times. Each time the processor added the value 10 to one register, it would increase by 1 the value contained in another register. After each addition, the processor would then check the second register to see if it contained the value 5. If it did, the processor would know that it had completed the operation—the value in the second register would be the product of the multiplication operation. Similarly, division would be treated as a series of subtractions.

New processors have more complex mathematical operations built into their instruction set and can perform them without such acrobatics. The Intel Pentium microprocessor has two duplicate sets of registers that allow it to perform two mathematical operations at the same time.

How Machine Language Uses Registers

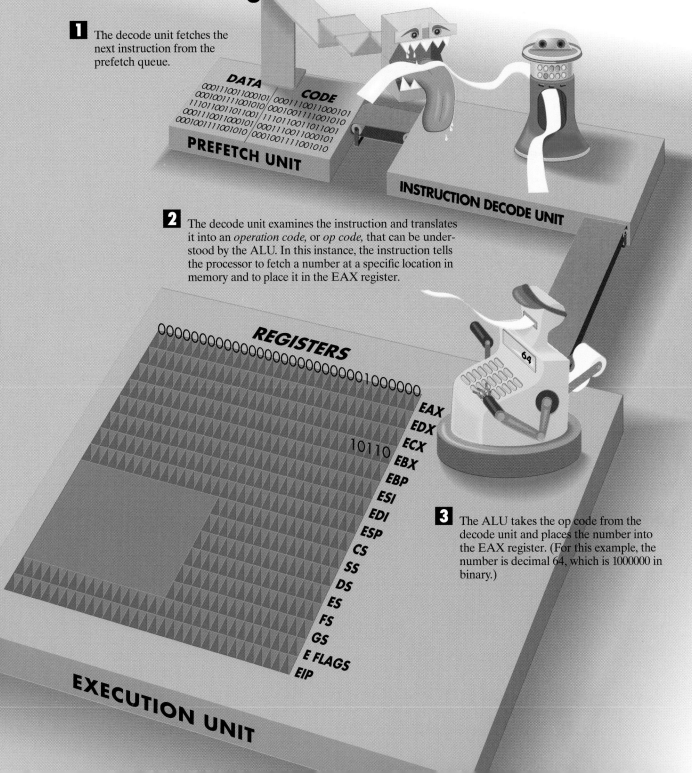

1 The decode unit fetches the next instruction from the prefetch queue.

DATA

CODE

PREFETCH UNIT

INSTRUCTION DECODE UNIT

2 The decode unit examines the instruction and translates it into an *operation code*, or *op code*, that can be understood by the ALU. In this instance, the instruction tells the processor to fetch a number at a specific location in memory and to place it in the EAX register.

REGISTERS

EAX
EDX
ECX
EBX
EBP
ESI
EDI
ESP
CS
SS
DS
ES
FS
GS
E FLAGS
EIP

3 The ALU takes the op code from the decode unit and places the number into the EAX register. (For this example, the number is decimal 64, which is 1000000 in binary.)

EXECUTION UNIT

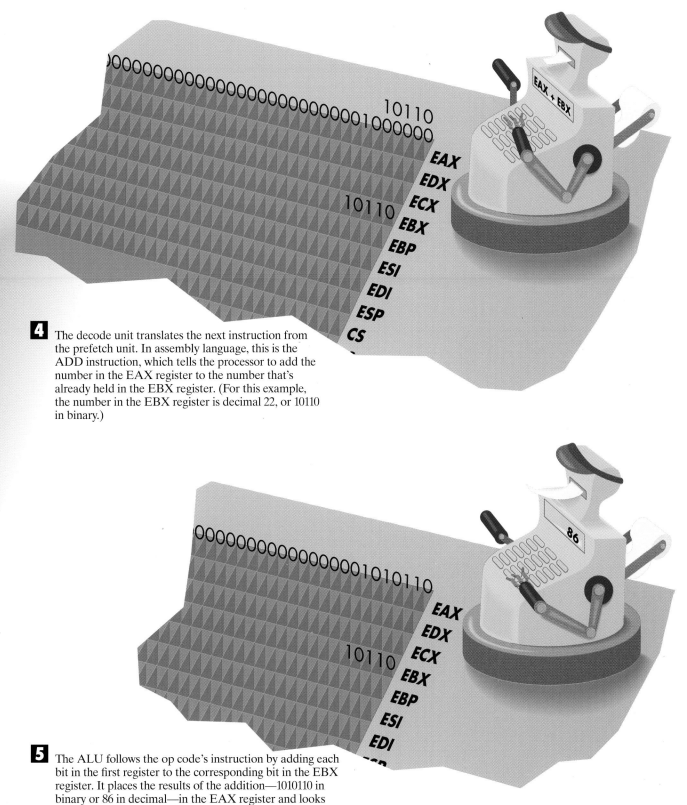

4 The decode unit translates the next instruction from the prefetch unit. In assembly language, this is the ADD instruction, which tells the processor to add the number in the EAX register to the number that's already held in the EBX register. (For this example, the number in the EBX register is decimal 22, or 10110 in binary.)

5 The ALU follows the op code's instruction by adding each bit in the first register to the corresponding bit in the EBX register. It places the results of the addition—1010110 in binary or 86 in decimal—in the EAX register and looks for the next op code from the decode unit.

How Programming Languages Translate Ideas into Software

PROGRAMMING LANGUAGES VARY in their command words and *syntax*, the way in which commands are constructed. For example, to assign the value 3 to a variable *X*, BASIC uses the command X = 3. Assembly language accomplishes the same thing by assigning the value to the AX register with the command MOV AX,3. Some languages may require several commands to achieve the effect another language accomplishes with a single command.

But regardless of the specific commands and syntax used by different programming languages, they all have in common certain abilities. They must obtain input from computer users and be able to manipulate that information. They must display output on the computer monitor or send it to a printer. They must read and write disk files. And they must be able to perform different tasks under different circumstances—this is the feature that accounts most for programming languages' power and diversity.

Typically, when a user types information into a program, it is stored as a *variable*. As the term suggests, the information a variable stores can vary from one instance to another. Programs on their own are also capable of storing in variables the information that is based on the results of a calculation or manipulation of data.

Once a program has information in a variable, it can manipulate it with commands that perform mathematical operations on numbers or parse text strings. *Parsing* is the joining, deletion, or extraction of some of the text characters in order to convert them into units understood by machine language. A *string* is another term for the contents of a variable. You can have math strings also, but most often, the term refers to an uninterrupted collection of alphanumeric and punctuation characters. Through parsing, a program can locate, for example, the spaces in the name "Phineas T. Fogg"; determine which parts of the string make up the first name, the middle initial, and the last name; and assign each segment to a separate variable. A typical manipulation command would be X = 2 + 2, which results in the variable *X* having the value 4. If that command is then followed by X = X + 1, the new value of *X* would be 5. The command X = "New" + " " + "York" assigns the string "New York" to variable *X*.

Although programs can rely on the BIOS to perform many of the input and output functions—such as recognizing keystrokes, displaying keystrokes on the screen, sending data through the parallel and serial ports, reading and writing to RAM, and reading and writing disk files—the programming language still must have commands to use the BIOS services. Consider the following series of BASIC commands:

```
OPEN "FOO" FOR OUTPUT AS #1
WRITE #1, "This is some text."
CLOSE #1
```

These commands create a file named FOO that contains the text in quotes, *This is some text*. The language Pascal does the same with these commands:

```
Assign (TextVariable, "FOO");
WriteLn (TextVariable, "This is some text.");
Close (TextVariable);
```

And because a program hardly ever proceeds in a straight line from start to finish, there are commands that tell the computer to branch to different parts of the program to run other programs. In BASIC, the command GOTO causes the execution to move to another part of the program. Assembly language does the same with the command JMP (short for *jump*).

These functions are fundamental—mechanical and unexciting necessities. More fascinating are the logic functions of the programming languages. There's not enough room here to discuss all of them, but let's look at three that demonstrate the subtle distinctions programs can make to suit different situations. The exact nomenclature and structure of the commands may vary from one language to another; the ones we use here are generic.

When a program needs to change what it's doing because a particular condition exists, it can use *"if...then..."* The program checks to see if a certain condition is true, and if it is, the program then performs a certain command. For example, *if* the state is Texas, *then* the program uses the abbreviation *TX* to address a letter.

But what if a program needs to perform some action repeatedly until a specific condition occurs? There are a couple of ways to accomplish that, each with a subtle but significant difference.

Using *"while...do (some command)..."* the program first checks if a certain condition is true, and if it is, performs a series of commands that ends with the program looping back to check if the condition still exists. For example, the program would use some variable—we'll call it *counter*—that keeps track of how many times a command is performed. As long as a variable named *counter* is less than 10, the program moves the cursor down one line, adds 1 to the number already contained in *counter*, and loops back to check the new value in *counter*. Once the value reaches 10, the execution of the software branches to another part of the program.

Using *"if...do (some command)...,"* the program first performs a command and then checks to see if a certain condition is true—the opposite of the order in a "while...do..." structure. If it is true, the program performs another command, usually one that leads the execution to another section of the program. If the condition is false, the program adds 1 to *counter* and performs the first command again. For example, when a variable named *counter* is equal to 10, the program branches to another action. Otherwise, it moves the cursor down one line, adds 1 to *counter*, and checks the new value in *counter*.

The differences between "while...do..." and "if...do..." illustrate issues a programmer must consider when writing software. In the example above, if the initial value of *counter* is 10 and the program is using the "while...do..." logic, the cursor will not move down a line even once. But if the program is using the "if...do..." structure, the cursor will move down one line before it finds out that *counter* is equal to 10. The "if...do..." structure will always perform the command in question at least once; that's not true of "while...do..."

To get an idea of how programs are written, we'll look at a *flow chart*—a kind of map sometimes used by programmers to lay out the logical connections among different sections of the program code. We'll use as an example a type of game that was popular in the days when text-only PCs were plentiful—an "adventure game." In such games, the user types in elementary commands, such as "Go east," "Go north," "Take knife," and "Hit monster." Our example is oversimplified and takes into account only one small portion of such a game. As such, it gives you an idea of how many commands and how much programming logic go into even the simplest code. In our adventure, the player is already on the balcony of a castle turret...

The Flow of a Program

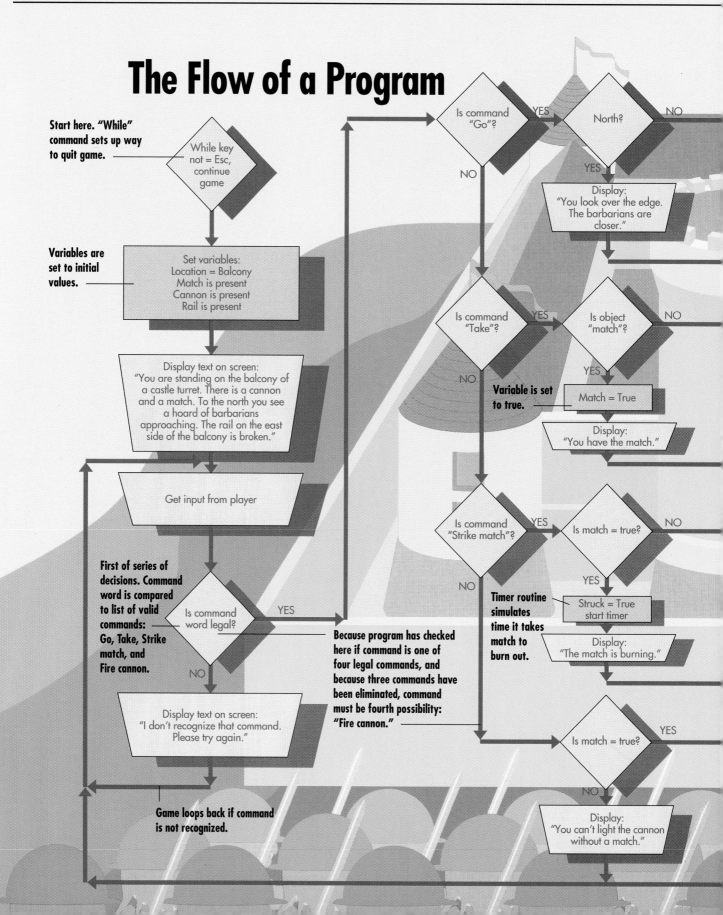

Start here. "While" command sets up way to quit game.

While key not = Esc, continue game

Variables are set to initial values.

Set variables:
Location = Balcony
Match is present
Cannon is present
Rail is present

Display text on screen:
"You are standing on the balcony of a castle turret. There is a cannon and a match. To the north you see a hoard of barbarians approaching. The rail on the east side of the balcony is broken."

Get input from player

First of series of decisions. Command word is compared to list of valid commands: Go, Take, Strike match, and Fire cannon.

Is command word legal?

YES

NO

Display text on screen:
"I don't recognize that command. Please try again."

Game loops back if command is not recognized.

Because program has checked here if command is one of four legal commands, and because three commands have been eliminated, command must be fourth possibility: "Fire cannon."

Is command "Go"?   YES   North?   NO

NO

YES

Display:
"You look over the edge. The barbarians are closer."

Is command "Take"?   YES   Is object "match"?   NO

NO

YES

Variable is set to true.   Match = True

Display:
"You have the match."

Is command "Strike match"?   YES   Is match = true?   NO

NO

YES

Timer routine simulates time it takes match to burn out.   Struck = True start timer

Display:
"The match is burning."

Is match = true?   YES

NO

Display:
"You can't light the cannon without a match."

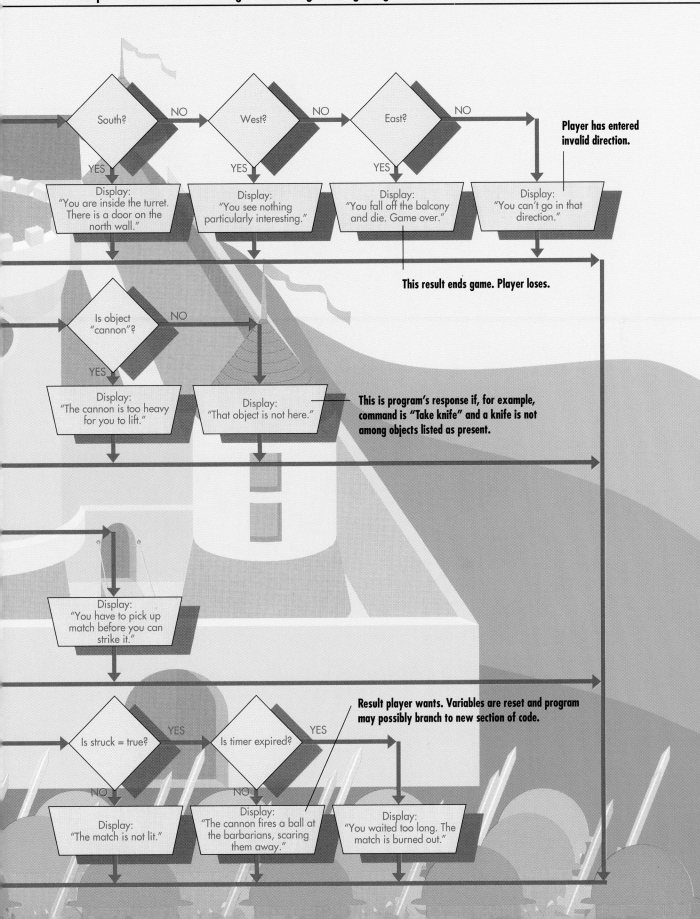

South? —NO→ West? —NO→ East? —NO→ **Player has entered invalid direction.**

YES ↓ | YES ↓ | YES ↓

Display: "You are inside the turret. There is a door on the north wall."

Display: "You see nothing particularly interesting."

Display: "You fall off the balcony and die. Game over."

Display: "You can't go in that direction."

This result ends game. Player loses.

Is object "cannon"? —NO→

YES ↓

Display: "The cannon is too heavy for you to lift."

Display: "That object is not here."

This is program's response if, for example, command is "Take knife" and a knife is not among objects listed as present.

Display: "You have to pick up match before you can strike it."

Result player wants. Variables are reset and program may possibly branch to new section of code.

Is struck = true? —YES→ Is timer expired? —YES→

NO ↓ | NO ↓

Display: "The match is not lit."

Display: "The cannon fires a ball at the barbarians, scaring them away."

Display: "You waited too long. The match is burned out."

How Language Interpreters
and Compilers Work

THE PROGRAMMING LANGUAGES that we humans can read are foreign to your PC's processor. Before your computer can read the instructions written in a programming language, they must be translated into the machine language that the computer's processor understands.

There are two ways to perform the translation: on the fly or permanently. The first method is used by language interpreters; the second is used by language compilers. In the early 1980s, there were a few commercially produced programs that used the BASIC interpreter, which was a part of the MS-DOS operating system, but today, most serious software is compiled.

Today, you will still encounter interpreters in two situations: if you use BASIC—which is not compiled except in some professional variations—to write your own programs, and any time you run a *batch file*, a miniprogram that lets you feed instructions to the DOS command interpreter.

If you've ever written a batch file or even modified your AUTOEXEC.BAT file, you can consider yourself at least a novice programmer. Batch language is looked down upon by professional programmers because it is so limited. It's true that batch language has a small set of commands and lacks such powerful features as the ability to manipulate variables. But used creatively, batch files can perform remarkably complicated tasks that simplify computing chores immeasurably.

BASIC, too, is rarely taken seriously by professional programmers. BASIC (Beginner's All-purpose Symbolic Instruction Code) was originally designed to be a simple language for teaching the principles of programming. It does not include features that the professionals consider essential for a real language—such as the ability to create *procedures*, which are segments of code that can be invoked simply by name. But you can perform virtually any operation with BASIC that you can with a more sophisticated language. The difference is in how you get to those operations—and the speed with which those programs are executed.

Programs written in interpreted languages are slow to execute because, in addition to handling the operations they are written to perform, instructions must be interpreted one at a time before each is executed. The interpretation adds more time to the process.

In addition, both batch files and BASIC programs require that an interpreter be on the system on which they're running. With batch files, that's no problem because the command interpreter is an integral part of DOS. Some form of BASIC is also supplied with DOS. Similarly, there are many programs written for Windows in Visual BASIC, but if you don't have a file called VBRUN100.DLL or VBRUN200.DLL, you can't use them.

Compiled programs, on the other hand, already have been translated from the *source code*—the original code in which they were written—into an *executable file*. Not only can an executable file run without the assistance of a separate interpreter, but it does so faster because it doesn't have to take time to translate the code.

It is not as easy, however, to make changes to compiled programs. In fact, if you don't have the source code, making any changes to a compiled program is a herculean effort undertaken only by programmers who have nothing better to do. Even with source code, however, changes are not simple since you must recompile the program after each set of changes. With a batch file or a BASIC file, you make the changes and then just run the program normally.

Most applications are obviously best written as compiled programs, but there will always be a place for quick-and-dirty batch files and BASIC programs. We'll look at both ways of converting source code into the machine code that makes your computer work.

How a Language Interpreter Works

1 When a batch file or a BASIC program is run, the interpreter for either establishes a small area in memory where it puts the name of the file and the current location from the start of the file, called the offset, each time it reads in a new line of instructions.

2 As the interpreter reads each line of the file, it compares the first word in the line to a list of valid commands. In some instances in a BASIC program, the interpreter will also recognize a variable at the start of a line.

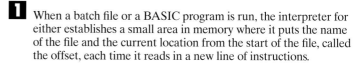

```
IF EXISTS FILENAME.EX
GOTO BRANCH
FORMAT F:
ECHO ANOTHER
:BRANCH
ECHO THE...
```

VALID COMMANDS

APPEND	GRAFTABL
ASSIGN	GRAPHICS
ATTRIB	HELP
BACKUP	IF
BREAK	JOIN
CALL	KEYB
FORMAT	LABEL
GOTO	LH

3 In a batch file, if the first word of a line is not found on the approved list, the interpreter will look for a .COM, .EXE, or .BAT file with a name matching the word. If none of these conditions are fulfilled in a batch file, or, if in a BASIC program, a matching command word or variable is not found, the interpreter generates an error message.

VALID COMMANDS

APPEND	GRAFTABL
ASSIGN	GRAPHICS
ATTRIB	HELP
BACKUP	**IF**
BREAK	JOIN
CALL	KEYB
FORMAT	LABEL
GOTO	LH

IF EXISTS FILENAM
GOTO BRANCH
FORMAT F:
ECHO ANOTHER
:BRANCH
ECHO THE...

10001110010101100010111

4 If the word is found on the list of valid commands, the interpreter executes the entire line, translating the command word along with the words that represent the parameters on which the command word is operating. These are turned into code *tokens*—shorthand abbreviations for instructions—that are passed to the microprocessor, which carries out the instructions.

INVALID DRIVE SPECIFICATION

OTO BRANCH
FORMAT F:
ECHO ANOTHER
:BRANCH
ECHO THE...

5 If any of the parameters are invalid, or if they attempt to perform a forbidden operation—such as copying a file over itself—the interpreter generates a syntax error message.

RAM

filename offset

6 Once the line has been processed, the interpreter retrieves the offset location of the next line and repeats the procedure. The exception to this is if a command, such as GOTO, branches execution to another section of the program.

How a Program Compiler Works

IF X>3 THEN Y=2
ELSE Y=Z+3

IDENTIFIER

VARIABLE	CONVERT
X	4
Y	2
Z	1

4 The result of the lexical analysis is a stream of tokens that represent everything of significance in the program—commands, pointers to variables, and numbers.

3 When the lexer finds a string of characters that don't form a reserved word, the lexer assumes that those characters stand for a variable. It assigns the variable a place in an *identifier table* that tracks the name and contents of every variable. Then, the lexer generates a token that points to the variable's position in the identifier table. When the lexer finds a string of numeric characters, it converts it into an integer and produces an integer token.

LEXER

REM SPACE CR

2 When the lexer comes across a reserved word or punctuation mark, it generates a code token.

IF 3

1 A portion of the compiler called the *lexer* reads the source code one character at a time, and performs a process called *lexical analysis*. As it reads characters, it tries to assemble them into *reserved words* (commands) or punctuation characters that it understands. The lexer discards spaces, carriage returns, and remarks included by the programmer to explain what sections of the code are supposed to do.

10 In a final stage, an *optimizer* inspects the code produced by the code generator, looking for redundancies. Any operation that produces results identical to those of the operation that precedes it is eliminated, making the program smaller and faster.

DUPLICAT
TRASH BI

WHILE TEMPLATE

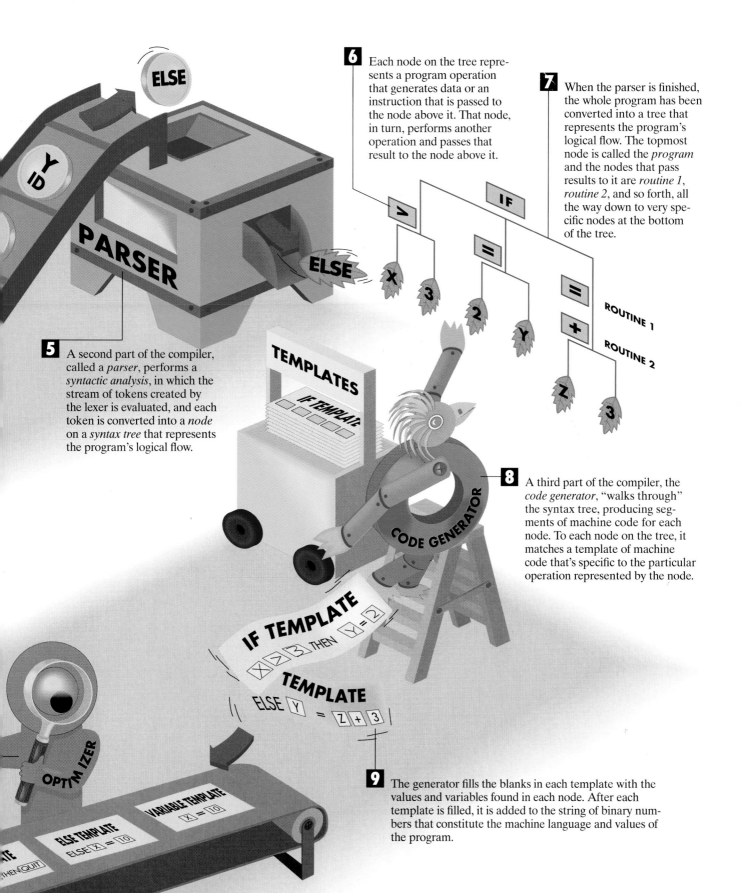

6 Each node on the tree represents a program operation that generates data or an instruction that is passed to the node above it. That node, in turn, performs another operation and passes that result to the node above it.

7 When the parser is finished, the whole program has been converted into a tree that represents the program's logical flow. The topmost node is called the *program* and the nodes that pass results to it are *routine 1*, *routine 2*, and so forth, all the way down to very specific nodes at the bottom of the tree.

5 A second part of the compiler, called a *parser*, performs a *syntactic analysis*, in which the stream of tokens created by the lexer is evaluated, and each token is converted into a *node* on a *syntax tree* that represents the program's logical flow.

8 A third part of the compiler, the *code generator*, "walks through" the syntax tree, producing segments of machine code for each node. To each node on the tree, it matches a template of machine code that's specific to the particular operation represented by the node.

9 The generator fills the blanks in each template with the values and variables found in each node. After each template is filled, it is added to the string of binary numbers that constitute the machine language and values of the program.

HOW DATABASES WORK

A DATABASE MANAGER is the most fundamental of all computer programs. What computers do best is juggle data—words, facts, numbers—and that's exactly what a database manager is designed to do.

If you're old enough to have visited a library that still used card files, you've worked with one type of noncomputerized database—one that illustrates perfectly the advantages of a computer database. Typically, libraries had three sets of card files: One set had a card for each book in the library, sorted alphabetically by title; a second set sorted the books by author name; and the third set sorted by subject matter. That arrangement made it easier for library patrons to find a book if they had only one bit of information about it. But it was a terrible waste of resources: The same information had to be repeated on cards in each of the three card files. Obviously, it would have been simpler and more efficient to have only one set of records that you could search by title, name, or subject matter. And that's exactly the advantage of a computerized database: It stores data that can be accessed and manipulated in many different ways.

Many programs that we don't think of as databases actually involve some form of database management. One reason that electronic spreadsheets such as Lotus 1-2-3 and Excel have become so popular is that, in addition to being able to calculate complicated mathematical formulas, they can sort and extract both mathematical and textual data. Accounting and inventory programs are specialized databases. Even word processors use database features in their spelling checkers and mail-merge operations.

But the databases we'll look at here are those dedicated exclusively to the manipulation of data—database managers exemplified by dBASE-compatible programs. The range of tasks a database manager can perform varies with the complexity of the program. But in general, they all do these jobs:

- Database managers let you define the type of data you want to store—alphanumeric or numeric, for example. They also define a format that aids in retrieving and organizing the data. A single piece of data may, for example, be limited to a certain length or to specific values.

- Database managers display on-screen forms in which data can be entered, edited, deleted, and viewed.

- Database managers carry out *queries,* which are searches for data that meets specified criteria, in order to allow you to retrieve certain subsets of the data.

- Database managers sort the data in different orders.

- Database managers perform calculations on the data. Not only do they do mathematical calculations, but they perform "if true" logic tests and join text data, allowing you to perform operations such as combining a person's first and last names.

- And finally, database managers present the data in a formatted, easy-to-read report.

How database managers perform these operations varies with the type of database. Many databases are designed for simple on-the-fly use. They provide ready-made tools and commands for performing relatively simple operations. More powerful database managers have their own programming languages that can be used to automate complex operations—operations so complex, in fact, that they are considered separate applications. A person may use an inventory program without realizing it was written in the programming language of a programmable database such as dBASE.

Database managers are distinguished from one another on another basic level. Some can manipulate only one table of data at a time; these database programs are called *flat-file* databases managers. Others can link data from several different tables. Although the exact definition is controversial, the term *relational* is generally used to describe such database managers.

In this section, we'll look at some of the fundamental operations performed by database managers: storing data; creating indexes that allow fast retrieval of data; and, in the case of relational database managers, linking data from different tables. The exact details vary with specific database programs; for our examples, we'll examine the methods found in the most widely used type of database managers, dBASE and its imitators, the *X-base* programs, which include FoxBase and Clipper.

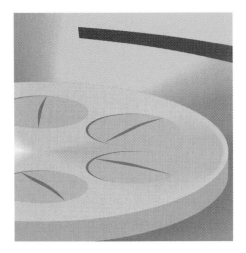

How Databases Store Information

MORE THAN ANY other type of software, database managers are defined by the ways in which they store information on disk. Even unassuming databases can create files tens of megabytes in size, and a database manager must be able to search, read, and change that data quickly if the manager is to be effective. Other programs, such as word processors, presentation graphics software, and electronic spreadsheets, perform their magic for the most part in RAM, where operations take place quickly. But database managers handle large amounts of data—too much to fit into memory all at the same time. They're forced to work with disk drives, the fastest of which are still immensely slower than the most sluggish RAM chips. Because the speed of the manager is determined by how well the data is organized on disk, it becomes all the more important that data be stored as efficiently as possible.

Different database managers use different file formats to store data on disk, but the most common formats are those designed for use with dBASE, the first database manager to become widely popular. The term *X-base* is used to describe any program that uses dBASE's file format and programming commands. dBASE's influence has been so pervasive that many rival programs fall under the X-base definition. And so much data has been saved over the years in the dBASE format that any database manager that wants to be taken seriously—even if it uses its own, different file format—must at least be able to read and write files in the X-base format.

Actually, there are two main types of X-base data-file formats. Both types of files contain *fields,* which are individual categories of information that make up a single *record*. For example, a database that tracks mailing addresses would have, typically, a separate field for the person's first name; one for last name; one for street address; and one each for city, state, and zip code. A single record would be a collection of one of each of those fields.

The more common of the two X-base file formats uses a .DBF file-name extension and is used for manipulating data that can be saved in *fixed-length* fields. In this type of record, each field is assigned a specific length at the time the database is designed. The designer of a database determines what is likely to be the longest piece of data that will be stored in a field. For some fields, this determination is no problem. A field for a middle initial, for example, is always one character long. For first and last names, however, it is more difficult to specify a field length.

When records are saved to a disk, they take up the maximum amount of space allotted to all their fields even if the data doesn't fill the fields. The designer, therefore, wants to keep fields as short as possible. If the designer makes fields larger than necessary, the disk files are bigger and take longer to search. If the designer makes fields too small, though, data may be truncated, resulting in such things as letters addressed to "Mr. Rumplestiltsk." Sometimes even when a designer thinks a certain field's length is a sure bet, circumstances change. For example, many databases designed for five-digit zip codes had to be redesigned when the post office began using nine-digit zip codes.

One way of avoiding the field-length problem, of course, is to use *variable-length* fields, which make up the other common type of X-base file format. These are identified by the file-name extension .DBT. Because there are no practical restrictions on the maximum length of variable-length fields—up to 16 kilobytes—they are often used to store such free-form materials as memos and other text. Some database managers use tables that consist only of variable-length fields. The trouble with such schemes is that variable-length files are more complicated to manipulate and don't lend themselves to such operations as alphabetical sorting and mathematical calculations.

We'll take a look at how both types of X-base records—fixed fields and variable-length memo fields—are stored on disk.

Fixed-Length Field Records

1 The beginning of a .DBF, fixed-field file contains information that defines the file's record structure—each field's name, data type (usually numeric or alphanumeric), and length. In addition, the structure might include information on the format of the data held in the field; for example, a field used to record dates might require the *MM-DD-YY* (month-day-year) format. A field can also be required to validate the information entered into it; for example, if the data entered into a validating state field is not one of the 50 postal service abbreviations, it will be rejected. A field definition can include a range of allowable data, a message to be displayed along with the field, and a default value for the field.

2 The rest of the .DBF file is data, laid down in one continuous stream. The locations at which specific pieces of data are recorded are determined by the lengths allotted to each field.

3 To find any given record, the database software calculates the location's offset through a simple formula: The record number multiplied by the total length of each record equals the starting point of the record. With the starting point calculated, the program reads the bytes beginning at that point in the file.

Record length = 52 bytes
× Record number =   3
Record starts at 156 bytes

4 To locate fields within each record, the program follows a similar process of calculating the number of bytes in the fields preceding the field it wants to find, and then reads bytes at the field's starting point.

5 To modify an existing record, the database software reads the record into variables in memory and lets you modify the information in these variables through an on-screen form. The software then writes the new contents of these variables to the database file.

6 As new records are added, they're simply stuck onto the end of the database file. The data itself is never reorganized or sorted in the file in any way. For that, the software uses indexes.

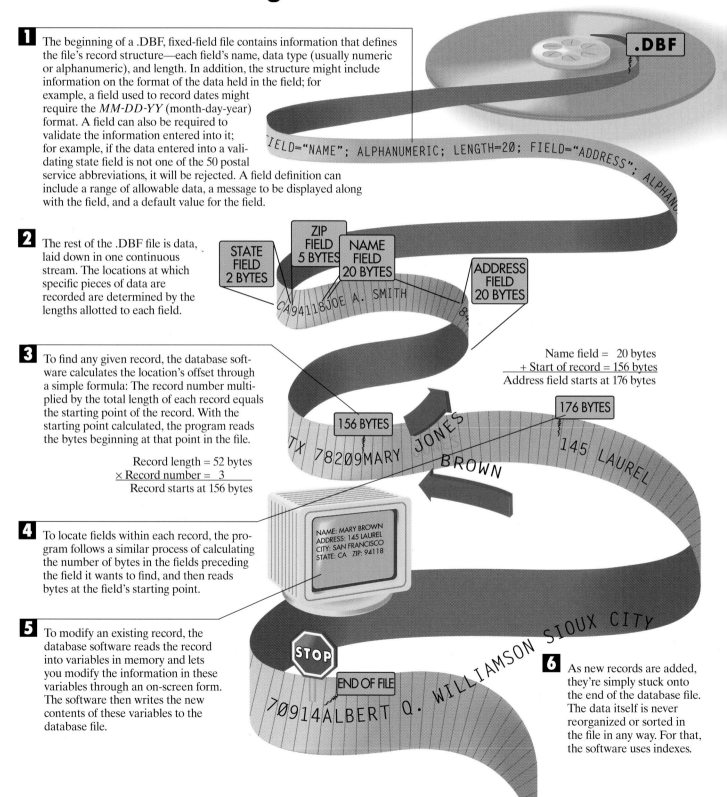

FIELD="NAME"; ALPHANUMERIC; LENGTH=20; FIELD="ADDRESS"; ALPHAN

.DBF

STATE FIELD 2 BYTES

ZIP FIELD 5 BYTES

NAME FIELD 20 BYTES

ADDRESS FIELD 20 BYTES

CA94118JOE A. SMITH

Name field =   20 bytes
+ Start of record = 156 bytes
Address field starts at 176 bytes

156 BYTES

176 BYTES

TX 78209MARY JONES BROWN   145 LAUREL

NAME: MARY BROWN
ADDRESS: 145 LAUREL
CITY: SAN FRANCISCO
STATE: CA   ZIP: 94118

STOP

END OF FILE

70914ALBERT Q. WILLIAMSON SIOUX CITY

Variable-Length Field Records

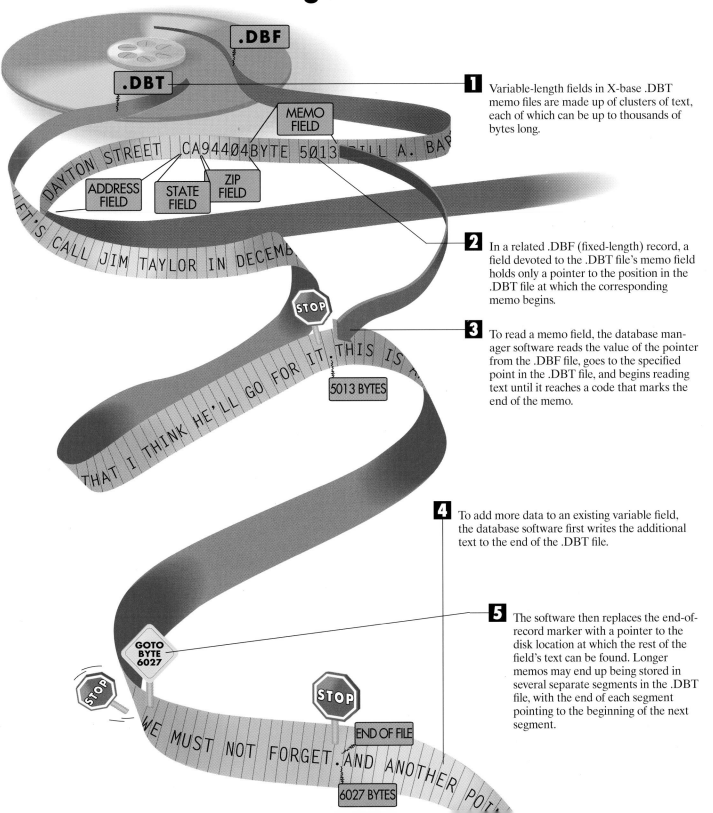

.DBF

.DBT

MEMO
FIELD

DAYTON STREET   CA94404BYTE 5013   BILL A. BA

ADDRESS
FIELD

STATE
FIELD

ZIP
FIELD

LET'S CALL JIM TAYLOR IN DECEMB

STOP

THAT I THINK HE'LL GO FOR IT. THIS IS

5013 BYTES

GOTO
BYTE
6027

STOP

WE MUST NOT FORGET. AND ANOTHER POI

STOP

END OF FILE

6027 BYTES

1 Variable-length fields in X-base .DBT memo files are made up of clusters of text, each of which can be up to thousands of bytes long.

2 In a related .DBF (fixed-length) record, a field devoted to the .DBT file's memo field holds only a pointer to the position in the .DBT file at which the corresponding memo begins.

3 To read a memo field, the database manager software reads the value of the pointer from the .DBF file, goes to the specified point in the .DBT file, and begins reading text until it reaches a code that marks the end of the memo.

4 To add more data to an existing variable field, the database software first writes the additional text to the end of the .DBT file.

5 The software then replaces the end-of-record marker with a pointer to the disk location at which the rest of the field's text can be found. Longer memos may end up being stored in several separate segments in the .DBT file, with the end of each segment pointing to the beginning of the next segment.

How Database Indexes Work

THE MORE INFORMATION you work with, the more helpful you will find a computer database to be. But the more information, the greater the strain on the abilities of even the fastest PC and the ablest software. That's where database indexes come in.

The principle of a database index is exactly the same as that of a book index. Instead of spending a lot of time searching every one of 1,000 pages for a term, you use the book's index—a relatively short but comprehensive listing of the book's contents as well as the pages on which they can be found. All you have to do is find the term in the index and then go directly to the specified pages—so it's much quicker. Substitute "database" for "book" and "record" for "page," and you'll understand the principle of a computerized index.

Database management software uses the index not only to search for specific records, but also when sorting data to arrange it in alphabetical or numerical order. During a sort operation, the records, which are probably scattered haphazardly throughout the database file, are not themselves rearranged on the disk; such disk-intensive activity would be extraordinarily time-consuming. Instead, the database manager uses information in the index to move from one record to another in the sorted order, giving the appearance that the order of the records has been changed.

As simple as the concept of an index seems, it's not that easy to implement an index in a computer database. An index is at its most efficient when handling redundant data, but, in many databases, the information in many field entries is unique. In a name field, for instance, there may be many *Jones*es and *Smith*s duplicating each other, but there also will be names like Symansky, Dvorak, Jillette, and Ziems—names that are likely to turn up in the last-name field only once. The greater the number of unique names, the larger the index, and the more time it takes to search. That means the index itself needs a technique to shorten search time. We'll take a look on the next pages at such a technique, called a *binary tree*.

Some database software requires records to have at least one *index key*, a field used for indexing, that contains unique data. Some database mangers automatically index every field, and some databases don't require any key field. But even if there is no explicitly unique field, each record has an implicitly unique number based on the order in which the record was written to the database. Only one record, for example, can be the first record; only one record can be the second record; and so on.

Since the order of the records never changes, the database manager can use the position number in combination with indexing to find records.

Indexes are not automatically a part of the information stored in most databases. They must be created based on the fields you're most likely to want to search, and you can create more than one index. The original indexing itself can be time-consuming but pays off later when you need to find records. Updating the index is a much shorter process if it's done regularly.

We'll look at how database indexes are organized and how they're used in a search. We'll also explore a technique used to make finding index entries faster, and how new entries are added to the index.

How a Database Indexes Records

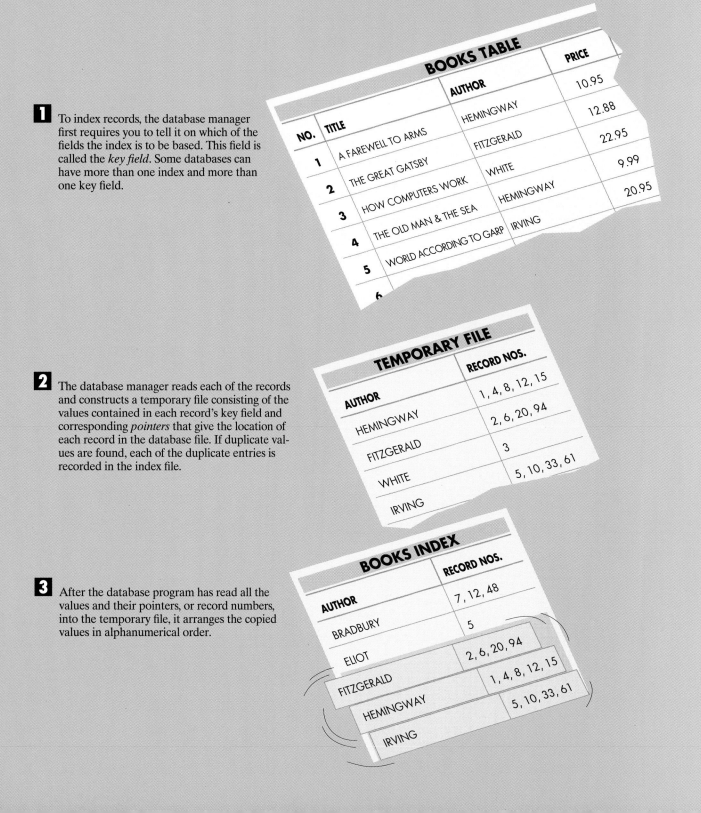

1 To index records, the database manager first requires you to tell it on which of the fields the index is to be based. This field is called the *key field*. Some databases can have more than one index and more than one key field.

BOOKS TABLE

NO.	TITLE	AUTHOR	PRICE
1	A FAREWELL TO ARMS	HEMINGWAY	10.95
2	THE GREAT GATSBY	FITZGERALD	12.88
3	HOW COMPUTERS WORK	WHITE	22.95
4	THE OLD MAN & THE SEA	HEMINGWAY	9.99
5	WORLD ACCORDING TO GARP	IRVING	20.95
6			

2 The database manager reads each of the records and constructs a temporary file consisting of the values contained in each record's key field and corresponding *pointers* that give the location of each record in the database file. If duplicate values are found, each of the duplicate entries is recorded in the index file.

TEMPORARY FILE

AUTHOR	RECORD NOS.
HEMINGWAY	1, 4, 8, 12, 15
FITZGERALD	2, 6, 20, 94
WHITE	3
IRVING	5, 10, 33, 61

3 After the database program has read all the values and their pointers, or record numbers, into the temporary file, it arranges the copied values in alphanumerical order.

BOOKS INDEX

AUTHOR	RECORD NOS.
BRADBURY	7, 12, 48
ELIOT	5
FITZGERALD	2, 6, 20, 94
HEMINGWAY	1, 4, 8, 12, 15
IRVING	5, 10, 33, 61

4 The database writes that ordered information to an index file that is structured as a *binary tree*. The binary tree, or b-tree, is designed to speed up the process of finding information in the index file. It's an upside-down tree in which each node has two (binary) branches. These branches break logical divisions of the index file into increasingly smaller halves. For example, A–M represents one of the first two branches of the tree, and N–Z represents the other main branch. A b-tree search lets a database search a million-entry index by checking only 20 sets of nodes rather than each of the one million nodes.

5 When the database manager needs to find records based on the key field, it checks successive branches of the b-tree. If the manager is looking for records whose key fields begin with an *I*, for example, the manager starts by looking down the main trunk of the tree, where it finds key-field values beginning with *M*.

6 Because *I* comes before *M* in the alphabet, the manager next looks at the key-field values halfway between *A* and *M*. There it finds values beginning with *G*. *I* comes after *G*, so the manager looks halfway between *G* and *M*, and so on, until it finds values beginning with *I*.

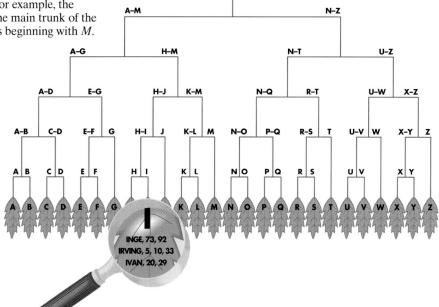

7 Eventually, the manager arrives at an end node—the leaf, so to speak—which contains a short, fixed number of entries (eight or so, depending on the program) and their pointers. It finds the entry it has been looking for and uses the pointer to locate the actual record in the database file.

INGE, 73, 92
IRVING, 5, 10, 33
IVAN, 20, 29
IVY, 121, 134

8 To reindex the database after new records have been added to the database, the program puts each new index entry into a blank space under the proper "leaf" in the index's b-tree.

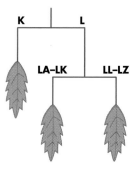

9 If there's no room under the leaf, then the software creates two new nodes under what had been the last node. For example, an *L* node would be divided into an *LA–LK* node and an *LL–LZ* node, each of which would receive roughly half of the parent node's information.

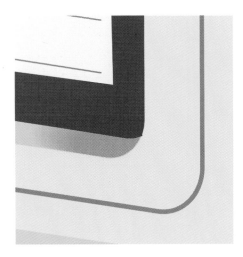

How Relational Databases Work

OF THE TWO types of databases—flat-file and relational—flat-file is more analogous to the hardcopy world. Most paper forms—your birth certificate, driver's license, marriage certificate, a job application, a 1040 form—are the equivalents of computer records in a flat-file database. All these forms contain pieces of information—such as name, spouse's name, parents' names, address, color of eyes, occupation—that would be referred to as fields in a computerized database. And in the computers that many organizations use to maintain these records, the resemblance in not merely figurative; they actually *are* fields. The information found on your driver's license is also found in a computerized database maintained by your state's Department of Motor Vehicles.

In fact, each of the hardcopy examples is most likely a record in some computer's database. But there's an inefficiency inherent in having the same information in so many different computer databases. If there's a change in the information for one of the fields the databases have in common, then each of the records must be updated individually. Consider what happens when you move to a new address: You have to individually change records kept in databases maintained by several separate organizations—your bank, your employer, the phone company, utility companies, the Internal Revenue Service, all your credit card companies, the Department of Motor Vehicles, and all those magazines you subscribe to. Wouldn't it be wonderful if you could change the address just once, and it would automatically be updated on all your records?

Real life is not nearly that convenient. In the computerized world, however, there is a way to maintain database records so that changes in one table can be applied throughout a collection of tables. That is the basic idea behind a relational database. There are different theories about what exactly constitutes a relational database, but for our purposes, let's define it as a collection of data tables that can be linked together through common fields. In the real-life example above, our address change, the common field in all the records would be your name. It is important for two reasons: It appears in each of the records, and it is unlikely to change—at least not very often—so it can be depended on to always be a common link among all the records.

The advantage of creating relationships among tables is that these relationships eliminate redundancy. You need maintain a person's address in only one of the tables; other tables that need that address can access it by using the person's name, the common element that appears in all the tables. By eliminating redundancy, you save space and make it easier to update your information. Just as important, your data is certain to be more accurate because there's no chance you'll overlook correcting the address in one of the dozens of tables in which it might appear. Once you make that change to a field in one table of a relational database, that change will show up everywhere the field is referenced.

Some PC database managers, such as Approach and Microsoft Access, automatically store information about relationships among tables along with the other database files. For example, Approach has a "view" file (.VEW) that contains information about the relationships among .DBF files. Other databases don't store relational information. If you use one of these, it's up to you to create any relationships by using programming or through on-screen menus.

Regardless of the method used, the results are the same and appear when you create a *report,* a selection of information drawn from the related tables and usually presented in a format designed to be read easily.

We'll look here at how tables are related and how information is updated and drawn from different tables as needed.

How Relational Databases Link Data

1 When a relational database is designed, care is taken to avoid repeating the same information in each of the tables—except for one field that is common to each table and that forms the basis for the relationship among the tables.

Common field

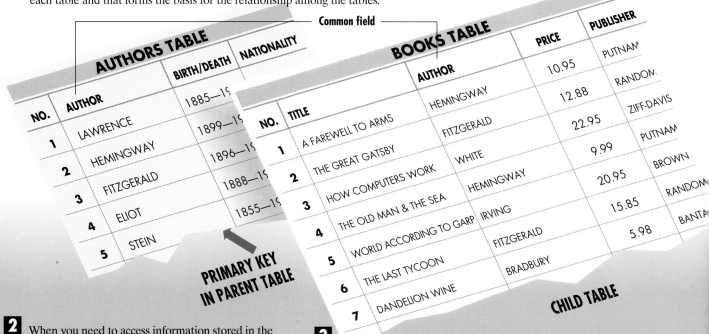

AUTHORS TABLE

NO.	AUTHOR	BIRTH/DEATH	NATIONALITY
1	LAWRENCE	1885—19	
2	HEMINGWAY	1899—19	
3	FITZGERALD	1896—19	
4	ELIOT	1888—19	
5	STEIN	1855—19	

PRIMARY KEY IN PARENT TABLE

BOOKS TABLE

NO.	TITLE	AUTHOR	PRICE	PUBLISHER
1	A FAREWELL TO ARMS	HEMINGWAY	10.95	PUTNAM
2	THE GREAT GATSBY	FITZGERALD	12.88	RANDOM
3	HOW COMPUTERS WORK	WHITE	22.95	ZIFF-DAVIS
4	THE OLD MAN & THE SEA	HEMINGWAY	9.99	PUTNAM
5	WORLD ACCORDING TO GARP	IRVING	20.95	BROWN
6	THE LAST TYCOON	FITZGERALD	15.85	RANDOM
7	DANDELION WINE	BRADBURY	5.98	BANTA

CHILD TABLE

2 When you need to access information stored in the database, you design a form or report that displays the fields that hold the information you want to retrieve. In this example, you want to obtain information about authors and their books.

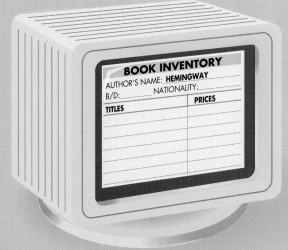

3 The Authors table contains the name, nationality, year of birth, and year of death of each of several authors. The Books table contains the titles, publisher names, prices, and author names for books. The Author field in the Authors table is the *primary key* for the relationship between the tables. A primary key must be a unique field in the *parent table*—that is, it must identify only a single record in that table. The Books table in this example is called the *child table*. The Author field is also a part of the Books table, but in that table, it is not unique: The same name can appear in several records. (One way to remember the terms is to recall that a parent table can be related to several children, but a child table has only one mother (parent).)

4 The form you design for this example specifies several fields from the Authors table, so the software finds that table, pulls out the contents of those fields for the current record, and displays them on screen.

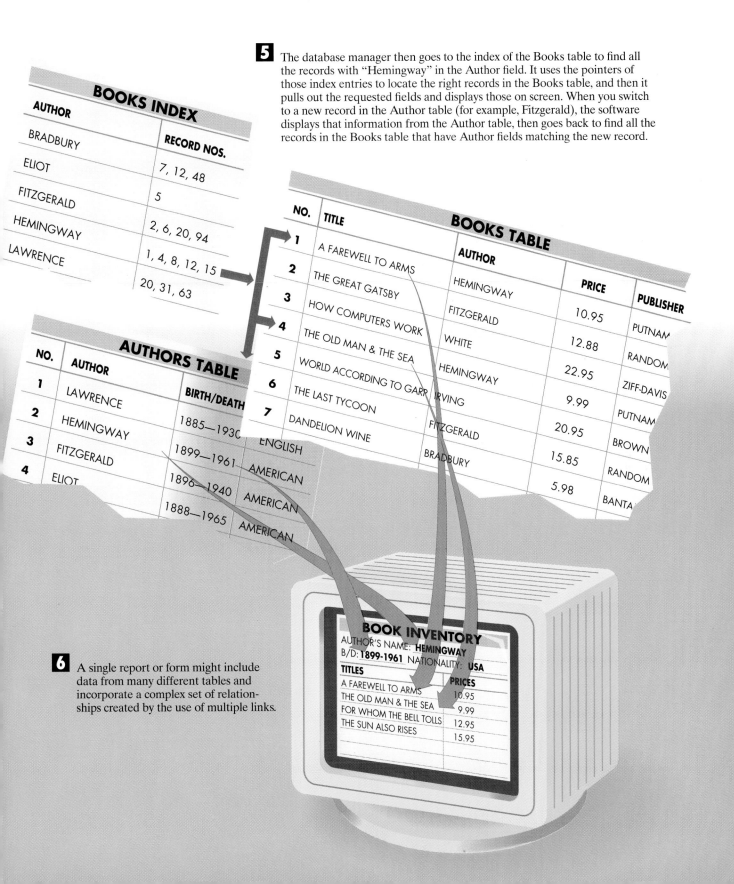

5 The database manager then goes to the index of the Books table to find all the records with "Hemingway" in the Author field. It uses the pointers of those index entries to locate the right records in the Books table, and then it pulls out the requested fields and displays those on screen. When you switch to a new record in the Author table (for example, Fitzgerald), the software displays that information from the Author table, then goes back to find all the records in the Books table that have Author fields matching the new record.

BOOKS INDEX

AUTHOR	RECORD NOS.
BRADBURY	
ELIOT	7, 12, 48
FITZGERALD	5
HEMINGWAY	2, 6, 20, 94
LAWRENCE	1, 4, 8, 12, 15
	20, 31, 63

BOOKS TABLE

NO.	TITLE	AUTHOR	PRICE	PUBLISHER
1	A FAREWELL TO ARMS			
2	THE GREAT GATSBY	HEMINGWAY		
3	HOW COMPUTERS WORK	FITZGERALD	10.95	PUTNAM
4	THE OLD MAN & THE SEA	WHITE	12.88	RANDOM
5	WORLD ACCORDING TO GARP	HEMINGWAY	22.95	ZIFF-DAVIS
6	THE LAST TYCOON	IRVING	9.99	PUTNAM
7	DANDELION WINE	FITZGERALD	20.95	BROWN
		BRADBURY	15.85	RANDOM
			5.98	BANTA

AUTHORS TABLE

NO.	AUTHOR	BIRTH/DEATH	
1	LAWRENCE		ENGLISH
2	HEMINGWAY	1885—1930	AMERICAN
3	FITZGERALD	1899—1961	AMERICAN
4	ELIOT	1896—1940	AMERICAN
		1888—1965	AMERICAN

6 A single report or form might include data from many different tables and incorporate a complex set of relationships created by the use of multiple links.

BOOK INVENTORY

AUTHOR'S NAME: **HEMINGWAY**
B/D: **1899-1961** NATIONALITY: **USA**

TITLES	PRICES
A FAREWELL TO ARMS	10.95
THE OLD MAN & THE SEA	9.99
FOR WHOM THE BELL TOLLS	12.95
THE SUN ALSO RISES	15.95

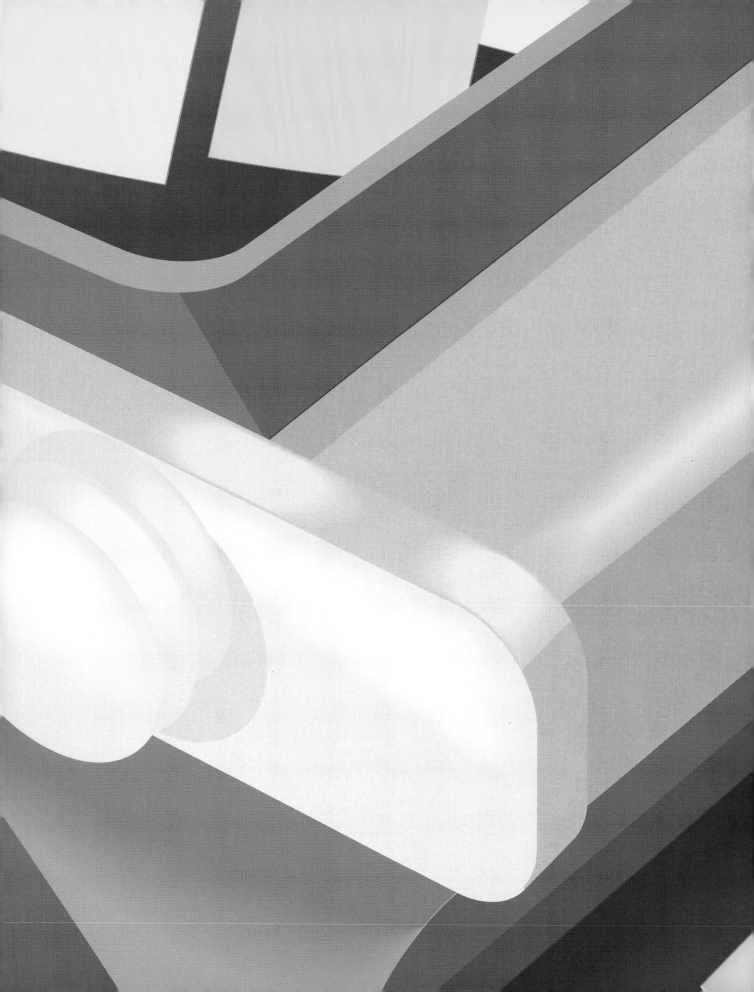

HOW SPREADSHEET SOFTWARE WORKS

4

CONTENTS

A PROGRAM CALLED VisiCalc is responsible for the fact that you're using a personal computer today. The early PCs—by today's standards, wimpy machines—made by Radio Shack, Apple, and Commodore, were mostly the playthings of electronics hobbyists. The mere fact that these hobbyists could buy a functioning, *real* computer was enough in itself to satisfy their experimental urges. The computer didn't have to do anything really useful, as the big mainframe computers did.

Then two young men named Dan Bricklin and Bob Frankston wrote a software program called VisiCalc, and the direction of the personal computer changed radically. Suddenly there was a real, practical reason to buy a PC. Running on the Apple II, VisiCalc was an electronic version of what accountants, department managers, bankers, and financial officers had been staring at on paper for ages: the spreadsheet.

In both its paper and computerized forms, the spreadsheet is simply a grid of vertical and horizontal lines into which labels and numbers can be entered to keep track of all sorts of numerical records, usually financial. But there is an important difference between the paper and electronic versions. On paper, to enter the sum of a long column of numbers, you have to do it manually or with the aid of a calculator, and then pencil in the result. If any of the numbers in the column change, you have to pull out the calculator and do the whole job over again. With an electronic spreadsheet, you can enter a formula that represents the sum of that same column of numbers, and the computer program will do the calculation and enter the result in the proper position on the grid. If the numbers change later, the electronic spreadsheet will automatically recalculate the formula and enter the new sum.

If the spreadsheet did nothing more than such simple calculations, it would still be a great saver of time and labor. But it actually does much more complicated tasks. Complex mathematical formulas are reduced to a few formula commands. Also, various *cells*—the rectangles formed by the grid's lines—can be linked so the results of one calculation become an element in a formula elsewhere. A change in the data in one cell can cascade in seconds through hundreds of calculations scattered among thousands of cells.

Imaginative business people quickly saw how this new computer program was a real business tool that justified the cost of personal computers. Not that they could always easily buy PCs—computer-related purchases in the late 1970s were controlled by MIS, or *management information system*, departments. The people in those departments—caretakers of huge mainframes—still considered personal computers to be mere toys. As a result, creative workers bought PCs with purchase orders that identified the computers as electric typewriters or copying machines. The demand for PCs created a market for programmers, who in turn created database managers, word processors, and other software that generated, in an upward spiral, more demand for PCs.

Early electronic spreadsheets were significant in another way. They represented the first *graphic user interface (GUI),* a term reserved today for the way that Windows, OS/2, and Macintosh systems display programs. Compared to those modern GUIs, the first electronic spreadsheet was a crude but recognizable on-screen representation of the spreadsheet format that people were already using on paper. That fact made it simple for computer users to grasp how the electronic spreadsheet was supposed to work. In minor and major ways, the ability of software to mimic real-world tools has continued to be one of its greatest strengths.

One historical note: No one uses VisiCalc today. Although it broke important ground in the development of the PC, VisiCalc failed to keep up with the innovations of other electronic spreadsheets, such as Lotus 1-2-3, which added database and graphing capabilities to VisiCalc's number crunching. Similarly, the software you find most useful on your PC today will probably look ridiculously primitive in another decade, too.

In the next two chapters, we'll look at two of the fundamental operations of electronic spreadsheets: how they arrange all the data in their cells so that cells can be linked to one another, and how formulas are used to perform the spreadsheets' calculations.

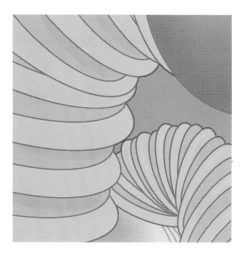

CHAPTER 11

How Spreadsheets Store Data

THE LOOK OF an electronic spreadsheet such as Excel, Lotus 1-2-3, or Quattro Pro is deceptive. The spreadsheet appears to be a large grid filled with text and numbers, each of the cells tightly abutting the surrounding cells. Behind that simple appearance, however, is a much more complex system aimed at conserving both memory and the processing power needed to make a spreadsheet work.

While you are working on them, spreadsheets are held entirely in memory. Setting aside enough RAM to hold the data that could be placed anywhere in a spreadsheet would require enormous amounts of memory. Spreadsheets can be thousands of rows deep and scores of columns wide, and cells must be able to hold long formulas and strings of text. To work with a spreadsheet that required memory for every possible cell that could contain data would mean reserving large amounts of RAM, much of which would not be used.

Early spreadsheets used a system that did require vast amounts of RAM. They used a *two-dimensional array,* which stacked the rows one after another in memory, and in which the cells were represented by a fixed number of bytes in a continuous line, much like the fixed fields in a database. To find a certain cell, the spreadsheet calculated its offset. Say you had a spreadsheet in which each cell took up *X* bytes of memory. To find cell B7, for example, the spreadsheet would multiply the number of the row by the number of columns in each row, add the number of the cell's column, and multiply the resulting number by *X*. The result would be the offset in bytes from the beginning of the array for the memory location where cell B7 begins.

Simple arrays, however, are inefficient because you can't allocate memory for an array as big as the entire workspace. It would be huge, and it would have a lot of empty space in it. Even if you limited the array by making it only as big as necessary—only out to the last row and column that actually hold data—there still might be blank rows or columns in there wasting space. And if you then added data to cells outside that range, the software would have to redefine the whole array to fit the new range, shifting everything around in memory to fit it into the new array. That's a lot of wasted effort.

Instead, modern electronic spreadsheets, such as Excel, use a system called *sparse matrix* that reduces the amount of memory you need to store a worksheet, allows faster calculations, and makes it easier for the spreadsheet to adjust as you add data to new rows or columns.

We'll look now at how an Excel spreadsheet works. Other spreadsheets, such as Lotus 1-2-3, are similar in principle but differ in some details; for example, Lotus 1-2-3 keeps track of cells by columns and Excel keeps track by rows. We'll look at Excel to see how it uses a sparse matrix to conserve RAM, how it allows you to add new data to a worksheet, and how it stores its data to disk.

How Electronic Spreadsheets Store Data

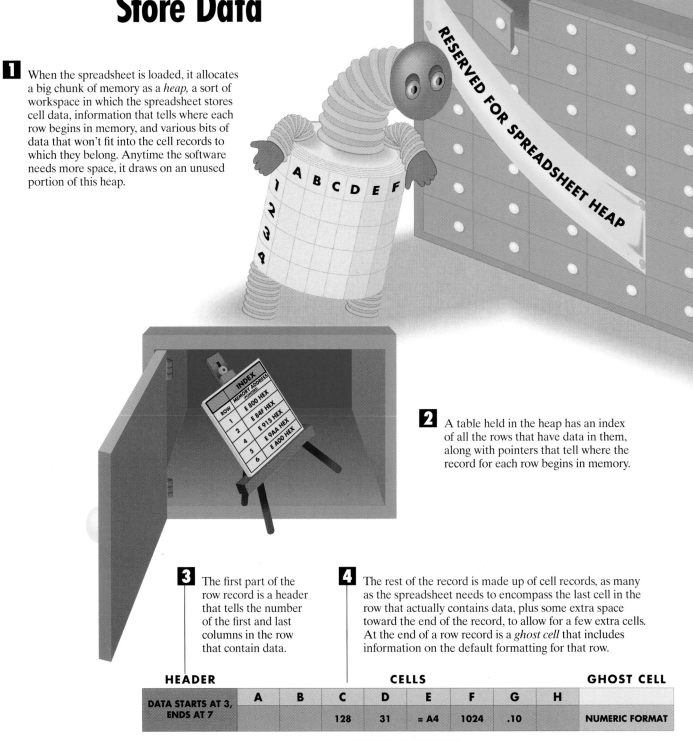

1 When the spreadsheet is loaded, it allocates a big chunk of memory as a *heap,* a sort of workspace in which the spreadsheet stores cell data, information that tells where each row begins in memory, and various bits of data that won't fit into the cell records to which they belong. Anytime the software needs more space, it draws on an unused portion of this heap.

RAM

RESERVED FOR SPREADSHEET HEAP

INDEX

ROW	MEMORY ADDRESS (POINTER)
1	E 800 HEX
2	E 84F HEX
4	E 915 HEX
5	E 9AA HEX
6	E A00 HEX

2 A table held in the heap has an index of all the rows that have data in them, along with pointers that tell where the record for each row begins in memory.

3 The first part of the row record is a header that tells the number of the first and last columns in the row that contain data.

4 The rest of the record is made up of cell records, as many as the spreadsheet needs to encompass the last cell in the row that actually contains data, plus some extra space toward the end of the record, to allow for a few extra cells. At the end of a row record is a *ghost cell* that includes information on the default formatting for that row.

HEADER			CELLS						GHOST CELL
DATA STARTS AT 3, ENDS AT 7	A	B	C	D	E	F	G	H	
			128	31	= A4	1024	.10		**NUMERIC FORMAT**

ROW RECORD

INDEX	
ROW	MEMORY ADDRESS (POINTERS)
1	E 800 HEX
2	E B00 HEX
4	E 915 HEX
5	E 9AA HEX
6	E A00 HEX
3	E C00 HEX

5 If you add more cells than can fit in the extra space, the spreadsheet software allocates a larger space for the row at another location in memory and moves the row data to that location. This method avoids the need to rearrange the entire spreadsheet.

6 If there are any blank rows—for example, between pages or tables—then the row index contains no reference to them. A row must hold data in order to be referenced in the row index.

7 If you start a new row or put data in an empty row in the middle of the worksheet, the spreadsheet software starts a new row record at the end of the data contained in the heap and adds information about its location to the row index.

8 To find cell G2, for example, the software first looks in the row index to find the pointer to the memory location where row 2 begins.

9 The software goes to that memory address and uses the information in the cell header to determine the address of the first cell that has data. Then it multiplies the number of bytes in each cell by the number of the column that contains the cell the spreadsheet wants to work with. The spreadsheet adds the product of the multiplication to the address where row 2's data starts, and the result is a memory address where the data contained in G2 begins.

EB00

X0 X1 X2 X3 X4 X5 X6 X7

HEADER

11 The next four bytes contain the cell's data if it's short enough to fit within four bytes. If it's longer, those four bytes contain a pointer to another memory location where the cell's data is actually stored.

1 BYTE 4 BYTES

| DATA TYPE: INTEGER | 1 | 0 | 2 | 4 | POINT TO CURRENCY FORMAT |

10 At the cell data's starting location, the first byte of memory indicates the type of data stored in the cell (integer, label, formula).

12 If the formatting for the cell differs from the default for the row as defined in the ghost cell, there is another pointer. This identifies a location in a "formatting table" that contains all the formats used in the worksheet. The format (boldface, flush left, currency, and so on) found at that address is applied on screen to the characters contained in the cell. In most worksheets, many cells share formats, so it's more efficient to use a formatting table than to repeat the format in each cell.

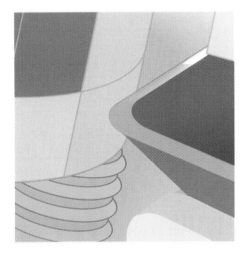

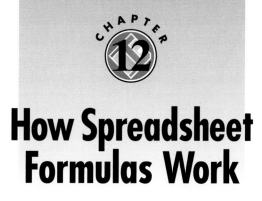

How Spreadsheet Formulas Work

T'S MORE THAN just the layout of an electronic spreadsheet that looks deceptively simple; the illusion extends to the cells themselves. If you place the spreadsheet's cursor on a cell containing a number, you may see a line at the top of the spreadsheet that shows something quite different. Instead of a number, there may be a mathematical formula that draws on data in other cells to produce the result you see in the cell.

One formula can lead to another cell, containing another formula leading to still another cell. When a spreadsheet is recalculated, there is an invisible flurry of activity as values are passed from one cell to another to another to another....

A spreadsheet such as Excel can have hundreds of *functions* that collapse complicated mathematical operations into a simple form of notation that even mathematical novices can use without understanding the underlying details. For example, to average the numbers contained in the cells ranging from B2 to B7, you *could* enter a long formula that adds B2 + B3 + B4 + B5 + B6 + B7, then counts how many cells from B2 to B7 have data in them, and then divides the sum of the values in the cells by the sum of the number of cells. Or you could enter the formula AVG(B2:B7).

The math behind a single formula might be formidable enough, but its complexity is minor compared to that of the logic required to calculate an entire spreadsheet in which dozens of formulas depend on each other. The spreadsheet program needs a way not only to keep track of all those relationships, but also to calculate them efficiently.

Here, we'll look at how formulas are stored in cells, how they are linked to one another, and how the spreadsheet executes them.

How a Spreadsheet Recalculates Formulas

1 When you type a formula into a cell, the spreadsheet processes the formula through a *mini-compiler* that converts the function names into a more efficient, tokenized format, in which functions are represented by specific numbers.

For example, functions such as SIN and COS are converted into specific byte values the spreadsheet recognizes as meaning "sine" or "cosine." The compiler also stores the formulas in *reverse Polish notation*, so that, for example, (3 + 2) * 10 becomes 3 2 + 10 *. This type of notation is more efficient, in terms of both space and speed.

2 The result of the compilation is written to a memory location reserved for that cell. The location also includes room for the result of the calculation, a pointer to the next formula in the spreadsheet, and a pointer to the previous formula. The pointers create, in effect, a list of those cells that contain formulas and save the program the time it would take to search every cell for formulas during recalculation. When you delete one formula, its pointer to a previous formula is used to reconnect the formula chain.

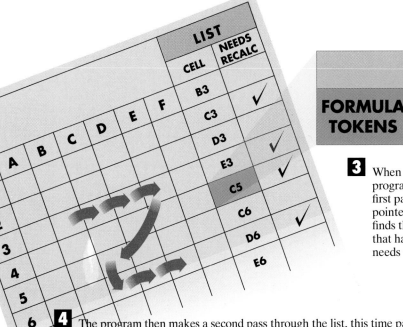

CELL C5		
FORMULA TOKENS	**ANSWER**	**POINTER**

3 When the spreadsheet is recalculated, the program saves work and time by making a first pass through the list created by the pointers of cells that contain formulas. It finds those formulas that depend on data that has changed, and marks each one that needs to be recalculated.

4 The program then makes a second pass through the list, this time paying attention to only the formulas marked for recalculation. For each, the spreadsheet determines if that formula depends on another formula that hasn't been recalculated yet. If so, it adjusts the cell's pointers and the pointers of connected cells so that the dependent formula moves to the end of the list. (This process pays off the next time the spreadsheet is recalculated—the program won't have to change the pointers again.) If the formula doesn't depend on any other formulas or if the formulas on which it depends have already been recalculated, then the software recalculates the cell immediately.

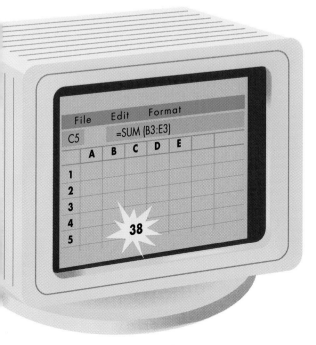

LIST	
CELL	NEEDS RECALC
B3	
C3	
D3	✓
E3	
C5	✓
C6	✓
D6	
E6	✓

6 The spreadsheet then moves to the next formula and repeats the process until it ends by finally calculating those formulas (earlier placed at the end of the list) that are dependent on other formulas.

5 To calculate a formula, the spreadsheet software feeds the data requested by the formula and the formula codes into a *calculation engine* that generates the answer and writes it to the part of memory allocated to hold information for that cell.

7 In some spreadsheet programs, such as Excel, the software updates each cell on screen as soon as it's been calculated. Other spreadsheets wait until the whole spreadsheet has been recalculated before updating the display.

NOTE If you've turned on a spreadsheet's automatic recalc feature, the spreadsheet is updated every time you make a change that affects any formula. How does it do this? When you create a formula, the spreadsheet software marks all the cells on which that formula depends by changing a notation in each of their records. In addition, it leaves hints in those cells about how to find the formulas that depend on them, a more efficient method than using pointers. When you make a change to any cell that's been marked in this way, the software finds the formula or formulas that are affected and recalculates them.

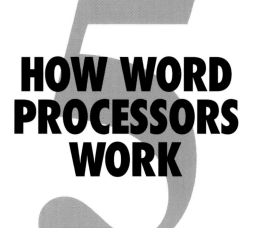

HOW WORD PROCESSORS WORK

PERSONAL COMPUTERS ARE used for word processing more than for any other application. That's not surprising when you consider how the business world communicates—with words. Whether through a company policy booklet, a letter to a customer, an annual report, or a memo to tell some boss to take this job and shove it, people in business communicate with words. But it is other applications—such as spreadsheets and databases—that actually benefit most from being computerized. Typing a letter on an IBM Selectric, after all, is relatively simple compared with sorting a few thousand records to produce, for example, an alphabetical list of every customer who lives in Arizona. However, not everyone uses a database or a spreadsheet. But everyone uses words, much of the time recorded in some form—on disk or on paper. And we want those words to be perfect. A slip of paper that's a crazy quilt of whiteout and penciled corrections may be an accurate record of words, but by today's computer-perfect standards it is simply not acceptable. Nor should it be. Word processors provide tools not just to record and print words but to make them attractive and more communicative.

The modern word-processing document has come a long way from the sloppier documents of the typewriter days, but the journey has been made slower by the fact that the technology has had to wait to be accepted by users. In the section on spreadsheets, we mentioned that the similarity of the on-screen spreadsheet to the paper one helped account for the immediate popularity of the electronic spreadsheet. The same is true of word processing, but computer users' insistence on maintaining that similarity kept word processors—until recently—in the basement of software innovation.

The first word processors weren't PC programs at all; instead, they were run on big mainframe computers and dedicated midsize minicomputers. Designed to emulate typewriters, they were *page-oriented,* which means they presented information on screen in a format that resembled a sheet of paper. A user had to move deliberately from one page to another, and if text were added that would push existing text to another page, the user had to make the word processor *repaginate* to redistribute the text.

These word-processing dinosaurs costs ten times what a PC costs today, and the only task they could handle was word processing. Needed to use a spreadsheet or a database? Then you had to resort to another computer system. Wanted to run a different kind of word processor? No way. These systems were dedicated not only to word processing but to a specific program that could not easily be replaced. The advent of the personal computer changed all that. PCs were more versatile, running many different kinds of applications, and software developers quickly gave users dozens of different word-processing programs to choose from, all of which could run on the same PC.

Even with the takeover of word processing by PCs, the software remained rooted in its typewriter heritage. For example, the technology behind word processing could, in theory, produce hard copy in any known typeface. But for the better part of a decade after word processing became popular on the PC, most documents were printed in a typeface called Courier—`which looks like this`. The only reason for using a typeface as unattractive and boring as Courier is that it matched what everyone was used to producing with typewriters. Even today, when Times Roman, Helvetica, and scores of other more attractive typefaces are available, many law firms—bastions of conservatism—still produce all documents in the Courier typeface that remains the standard for legal documents.

In the last few years, however, virtually all boundaries of word processing have been broken. It is quickly becoming commonplace for word processors to use a variety of fonts, to import spreadsheet data (or to have a built-in spreadsheet), to provide grammar checkers, drawing modules, thesauruses, dictionaries, and fax capabilities. Virtually anything you can imagine being printed on paper can be produced with a PC word processor.

And yet for all the new capabilities, the primary task of a word processor—producing words on paper—has remained unchanged. (The paperless office is still more an idea than a reality.) In the next two chapters, we'll look at the functions most crucial to this task: formatting text on screen in preparation for sending it to the printer, and using bitmapped and outline fonts to print hard copy.

How Word-Processing
Documents Are Formatted

BESIDES ITS ABILITY to make text changes easily and print a new copy of a document without rekeying every word, a word processor's biggest advantage is the way that it can *sculpt* text—shape the margins, mold the type (boldface for some, italic for others), and add such elements as headers and footnotes that flow seamlessly with the document no matter how it's cut and pasted. This sculpting is called *text formatting.* Much of a word processor's resources are devoted not only to keeping track of the words you type into it, but to recording how you want those words to appear on the screen and on the printed page. The details of how this is done vary with each word processor, but in general, there are two types of formatting: *in-line* and *property-oriented.*

In-line formatting is found most often in older, non-Windows word processors (although WordPerfect has done an excellent job of incorporating in-line formatting into its Windows version). It evolved from the capabilities of early printers and the methods software used to communicate with them. These printers had specific fonts built into them in the form of *bitmaps* that corresponded to ASCII codes. We'll look at bitmaps more in the next chapter; for now, suffice it to say that a bitmapped font is a specific typeface in a fixed size that can't be changed. *ASCII,* which stands for *American Standard Code for Information Interchange,* is a universally used system under which certain numbers—0 to 127—represent specific alphanumeric characters, punctuation marks, and printer actions. The use of ASCII codes makes it possible to transfer data from one program to another. An uppercase *A,* for example, is represented by the decimal number 65; a lowercase *a,* by 97; and a comma, by 44.

The printers also had specific abilities that were activated when the computer sent special ASCII control codes. For example, the ASCII number 10 tells a printer to advance the paper one line, and the number 12 tells it to eject the page or advance the paper to the next page. More elaborate codes tell the printer which bitmapped font set to use and can control the exact placement of text on paper. In-line formatting—whether presented on screen or on paper—consists basically of a stream of text interspersed with control codes.

Property-oriented formatting is normally associated with a *page description language* (PDL). A PDL abandons the idea of a stream of text and codes. In fact, it ignores almost entirely the controls and bitmaps built into a printer. In their place, the page description language takes control of all aspects of the printer, instructing it where to place each dot of ink or toner that makes up text and graphics.

How each method works depends on the *printer driver* used by the word processor. A driver is an extension to the operating system and is tailored to a specific piece of hardware, such as a Hewlett-Packard LaserJet III printer or a super VGA display. The printer driver takes the information provided by the in-line stream of data or the page description language and converts it into low-level commands recognized by the printer. (A screen driver does the same with the video adapter to display text on the monitor.) By working with different drivers, a word processor can work with the same document on a variety of displays and printers.

We'll look here at how these methods work. Although the trend, particularly in the Windows environment, is toward the use of page description languages, there are still millions of computers using in-line word processors, ensuring that that method will also be important for years to come.

How In-Line Formatting Works

1 When you type characters into the word processor, they are stored as ASCII codes, shown here as numbers, in a section of memory set aside for them.

N o w i s t i m e
4Eh 6Fh 77h 20h 69h 73h 20h 74h 69h

2 If new characters are inserted into the middle of existing text, the word processor adds the new text to the end of the preexisting text in RAM and sets up a pointer to keep track of the correct order in which the text should appear. When the document is written to disk, the separate sections of text are sorted out and written to the file in a continuous stream.

N o w i s t i m e t h e
4Eh 6Fh 77h 20h 69h 73h 20h 74h 69h 6Dh 65h 74h 68h 65h

3 A special section of the document, called the *header,* stores information about the file, such as the default font, margin settings, tab settings, and other data that is applied throughout the document unless a specific change is made.

LEFT MARGIN = 1" RIGHT MARGIN = 1.5"
DEFAULT FONT = 12PT. HELVETICA
LINE SPACING = 1 TAB EVERY .5"

N o w i s
4Eh 6Fh 77h 20h 69h 73h

4 When you tell the word processor to apply a special format to a section of the text, the word processor inserts its own code for that format at the beginning of the section in RAM. At the end of the section, it inserts another code that signals the end of the formatting. These codes usually are not displayed on screen.

RIGHT MARGIN = 1.5"
HELVETICA
TAB EVERY .5"

BOLD FACE ON

N o w BOLD FACE OFF i
4Eh 6Fh 77h 20h 69h

5 As you type text or scroll through a document, the word processor reads more text and formatting codes from RAM and processes them through a display driver.

6 If the word processor is DOS-based, the driver uses the PC's BIOS to translate ASCII codes to text. The BIOS matches a table of ASCII numbers to their corresponding bitmapped patterns of screen pixels, which are then lighted to form characters. A formatting code activates an alternative pattern built into the BIOS, causing the text to be displayed as bold or underlined. Only patterns that are built into the BIOS's table can be displayed, unless a word processor substitutes its own bitmaps. The BIOS cannot display illustrations, but it does contain simple graphic characters for drawing lines and boxes.

ASCII CODE	PIXEL PATTERN
41h	A
42h	B
43h	C

7 If the word processor has a graphical interface, the display driver ignores the BIOS and sends its own commands to the display adapter to light up the pixels needed to form text, lines, graphics, or any other on-screen element. There is no limit to what can be displayed using this method.

8 When the word processor sends text to be printed, a printer driver performs a similar function to translate text and formatting into the patterns of dots created by all printers, whether dot-matrix, bubble-jet, or laser. The exact process depends on whether a bitmapped font or a page description language is used. (See the next chapter.)

How Property-Oriented Formatting Works

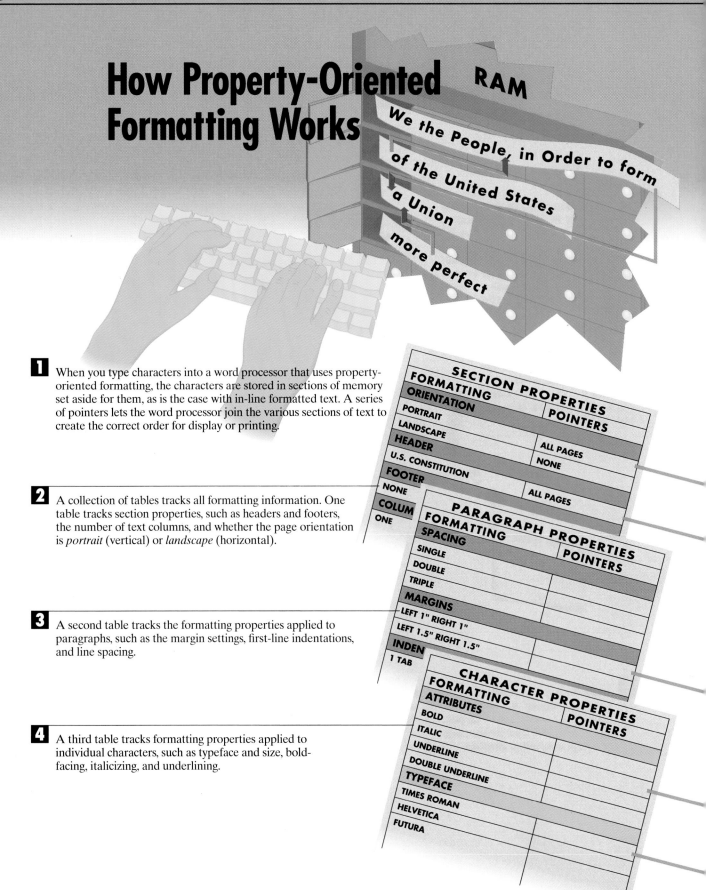

RAM

We the People, in Order to form of the United States a Union more perfect

1 When you type characters into a word processor that uses property-oriented formatting, the characters are stored in sections of memory set aside for them, as is the case with in-line formatted text. A series of pointers lets the word processor join the various sections of text to create the correct order for display or printing.

2 A collection of tables tracks all formatting information. One table tracks section properties, such as headers and footers, the number of text columns, and whether the page orientation is *portrait* (vertical) or *landscape* (horizontal).

3 A second table tracks the formatting properties applied to paragraphs, such as the margin settings, first-line indentations, and line spacing.

4 A third table tracks formatting properties applied to individual characters, such as typeface and size, bold-facing, italicizing, and underlining.

SECTION PROPERTIES

FORMATTING	POINTERS
ORIENTATION	
PORTRAIT	
LANDSCAPE	
HEADER	ALL PAGES
U.S. CONSTITUTION	NONE
FOOTER	
NONE	ALL PAGES
COLUM	
ONE	

PARAGRAPH PROPERTIES

FORMATTING	POINTERS
SPACING	
SINGLE	
DOUBLE	
TRIPLE	
MARGINS	
LEFT 1" RIGHT 1"	
LEFT 1.5" RIGHT 1.5"	
INDEN	
1 TAB	

CHARACTER PROPERTIES

FORMATTING	POINTERS
ATTRIBUTES	
BOLD	
ITALIC	
UNDERLINE	
DOUBLE UNDERLINE	
TYPEFACE	
TIMES ROMAN	
HELVETICA	
FUTURA	

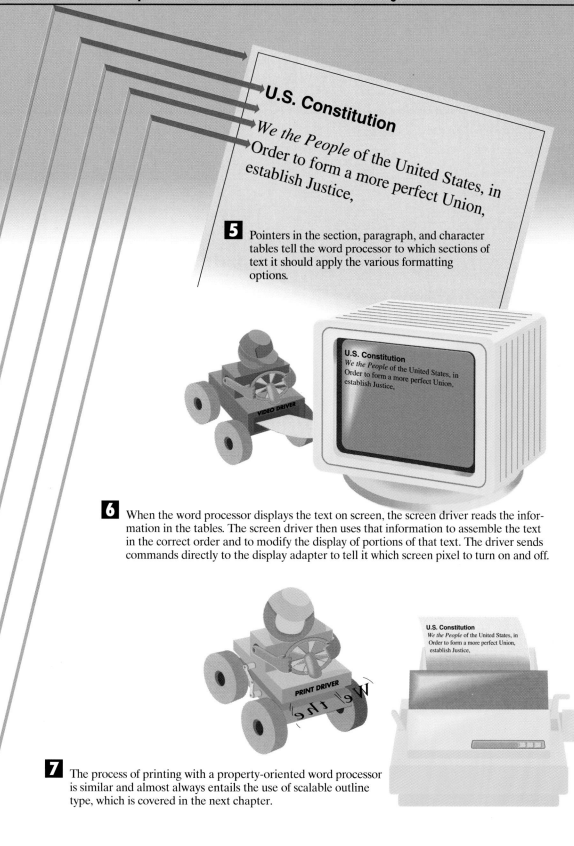

U.S. Constitution

We the People of the United States, in Order to form a more perfect Union, establish Justice,

5 Pointers in the section, paragraph, and character tables tell the word processor to which sections of text it should apply the various formatting options.

U.S. Constitution
We the People of the United States, in Order to form a more perfect Union, establish Justice,

VIDEO DRIVER

6 When the word processor displays the text on screen, the screen driver reads the information in the tables. The screen driver then uses that information to assemble the text in the correct order and to modify the display of portions of that text. The driver sends commands directly to the display adapter to tell it which screen pixel to turn on and off.

PRINT DRIVER

U.S. Constitution
We the People of the United States, in Order to form a more perfect Union, establish Justice,

7 The process of printing with a property-oriented word processor is similar and almost always entails the use of scalable outline type, which is covered in the next chapter.

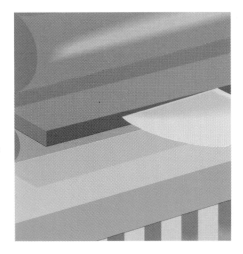

CHAPTER
14

How Fonts Work

T USED TO be that working with fonts in word processing was a simple matter. You had a choice of three—10-character-per-inch Courier, 12-character-per-inch Courier, or Line Printer, which is a small, particularly unattractive font handy for cramming a lot of spreadsheet or database information onto a single line. And, on some early dot-matrix printers, there wasn't even Courier. Instead, the printer used some typeface that was so crude that no one usually even bothered to name it. When dot-matrix printers finally were able to produce Courier—an imitation of the common pica type used on old manual typewriters—it was considered a great improvement.

Today, no self-respecting letter writer uses Courier, the word processing equivalent of the eight-track tape. We now have easy access to Times Roman, Helvetica, Garamond, Cooper Black, Optima, Bodoni, and scores of other typefaces. Gutenberg would be amazed. There are two ways to get all these wonderful fonts: through *bitmapped* or *outline* characters.

Before going any further, we ought to clear up a couple of terms that can be confusing: typeface and font. A *typeface* is any family of type, encompassing all sizes and attributes (for example, bold or italic are attributes). Times Roman is a typeface. A *font* is a typeface in a particular size with a particular attribute. Times Roman 10-point, Times Roman 10-point bold, and Times Roman 9-point are three different fonts that belong to the Times Roman typeface family.

A *bitmap* is a record in memory of the exact pattern of dots needed to create a specific character in a specific typeface, size, and style on paper (or on the screen)—for example, the pattern of dots that make up the 10-point Times Roman bold letter *A* illustrated on page 118. If you wanted the *A* to be in Helvetica, instead, or to be 9 points high or italic, an entirely separate bitmap would be required.

If you need to use more than a single typeface in a few specific fonts, bitmapped fonts have an inherent drawback—you have to have a lot of them, which takes up space both on disk and in a printer's memory. Using bitmapped fonts is like having separate cars for going to work, to the grocery store, to the shopping mall, and to take the kids to school. You soon run out of room in the garage. Wouldn't it be much better to have a single car that could adjust to going to different places?

That single car is the equivalent of *outline* type, which provides the second way to use different fonts. An outline typeface is no particular font at all. Instead, it is a formula—a template that can be modified to create, on the fly, different sizes and attributes of a particular typeface.

The advantages of outline types are that they take up less space on disk and in memory, and they provide virtually endless variations on the same typeface. Instead of storing each variation, you only have to store the formula for the typeface. When it comes time to use a particular font, your software passes along to the formula the size and attribute you want the font to have, and the formula churns out the pattern of dots the printer needs to create the required characters.

Bitmapped fonts have their place. They may be faster for older, slower PCs to use because the PC or the printer doesn't have to spend time translating an outline formula into a specific font. They can be convenient, too, because at least a few bitmapped fonts are provided with every printer; some of these collections are quite respectable and include specific sizes of Times Roman and Helvetica. If you have good bitmapped fonts, use them.

We're going to look at how a word processor uses both bitmapped fonts and outline type. We usually associate bitmapped fonts with dot-matrix printers and outline typefaces with laser printers. But keep in mind that the PC world is getting complicated—the distinctions between a hardware function and a software function are becoming blurred. Bitmapped fonts are built into all printers, but they can also be generated by software and downloaded to a printer's memory. Although we usually associate outline type with software—and particularly with Windows—some printers, especially laser printers, come with outline type capabilities built into them, and the process of churning through outline formulas can take place in either the computer or the printer. And although we tend to think of outline type only for laser printers and bitmapped fonts for dot-matrix printers, you can usually use either kind of font on either type of printer. In any case, these examples will give you an accurate picture of how both types of fonts work.

We've chosen to discuss this topic in a section on word processing because that is the application—along with desktop publishing—where fonts are most likely to be of importance. But particularly in the growing Windows environment, spreadsheets, database managers, and just about any other sophisticated program can take advantage of either type of font.

How Bitmapped Fonts Work

1 A bitmapped font is a specific pattern of dots that form a specific typeface's characters in a specific size and characteristic, such as bold or italic. The bitmap for a Times Roman 24-point *A* is different from the bitmap for a Times Roman bold 24-point *A,* and both are different from the bitmap for a Times Roman 14-point *A.*

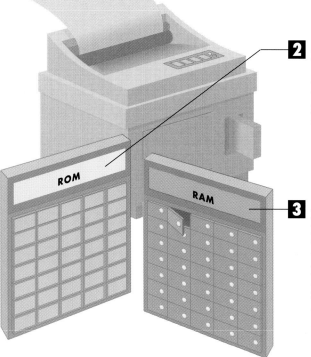

2 Most printers come with specific bitmapped fonts, such as 12-point Courier, stored in ROM chips on the printer's main circuit boards (*ROM chips* are read-only memory chips— their memory can't be changed). The standard bitmapped fonts can be supplemented by plug-in cartridges that contain other such fonts.

3 In addition to providing fixed bitmapped fonts in ROM, most printers also have several kilobytes of RAM that can hold other bitmapped fonts downloaded from the PC's hard drive to the printer. If the software sends more bitmaps than the printer's memory can hold at one time, different sets of characters are juggled in and out of the printer's RAM as they're required. When the printer is turned off, the fonts in RAM are lost and must be reloaded from the computer.

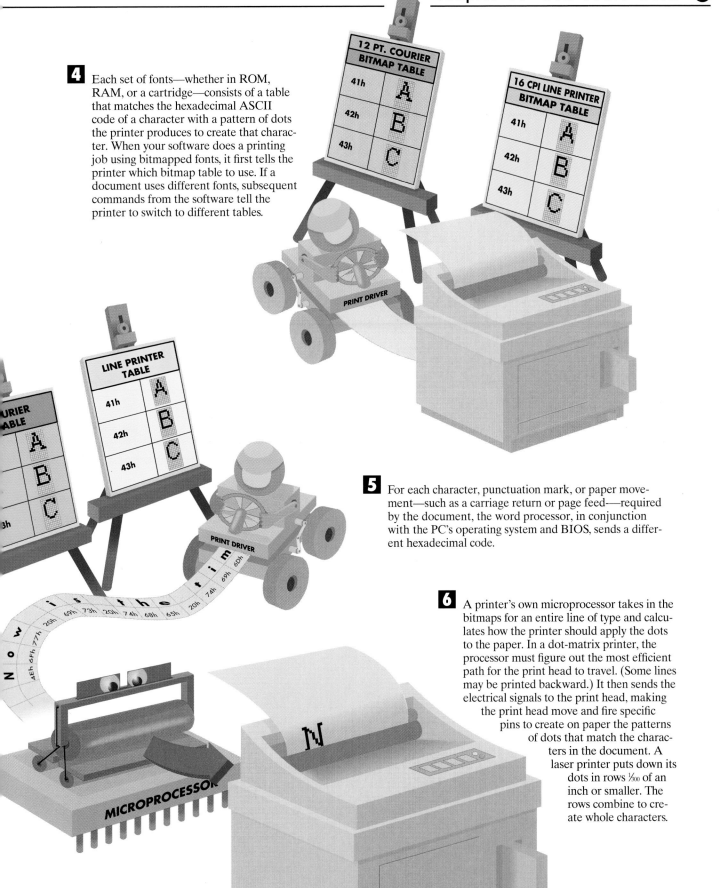

4 Each set of fonts—whether in ROM, RAM, or a cartridge—consists of a table that matches the hexadecimal ASCII code of a character with a pattern of dots the printer produces to create that character. When your software does a printing job using bitmapped fonts, it first tells the printer which bitmap table to use. If a document uses different fonts, subsequent commands from the software tell the printer to switch to different tables.

5 For each character, punctuation mark, or paper movement—such as a carriage return or page feed——required by the document, the word processor, in conjunction with the PC's operating system and BIOS, sends a different hexadecimal code.

6 A printer's own microprocessor takes in the bitmaps for an entire line of type and calculates how the printer should apply the dots to the paper. In a dot-matrix printer, the processor must figure out the most efficient path for the print head to travel. (Some lines may be printed backward.) It then sends the electrical signals to the print head, making the print head move and fire specific pins to create on paper the patterns of dots that match the characters in the document. A laser printer puts down its dots in rows ⅟₃₀₀ of an inch or smaller. The rows combine to create whole characters.

How Outline Type Works

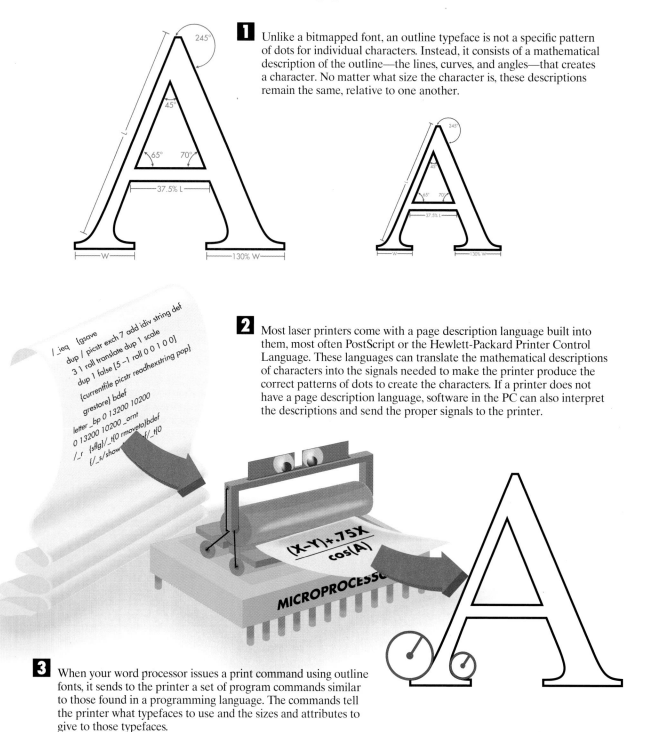

1 Unlike a bitmapped font, an outline typeface is not a specific pattern of dots for individual characters. Instead, it consists of a mathematical description of the outline—the lines, curves, and angles—that creates a character. No matter what size the character is, these descriptions remain the same, relative to one another.

2 Most laser printers come with a page description language built into them, most often PostScript or the Hewlett-Packard Printer Control Language. These languages can translate the mathematical descriptions of characters into the signals needed to make the printer produce the correct patterns of dots to create the characters. If a printer does not have a page description language, software in the PC can also interpret the descriptions and send the proper signals to the printer.

3 When your word processor issues a print command using outline fonts, it sends to the printer a set of program commands similar to those found in a programming language. The commands tell the printer what typefaces to use and the sizes and attributes to give to those typefaces.

4 The page description language plugs variables, such as point size, into the formulas for a typeface. Calculating a formula with those variables results in a specific set of instructions that describe the outline of a character; for example, "Create a horizontal line 3 points wide, beginning 2 points from the baseline and continuing at a 60-degree angle for 20 points…" The page description language turns on all the bits that fall inside the character's outline to produce a solid letter—unless a special fill or other shading effect is used.

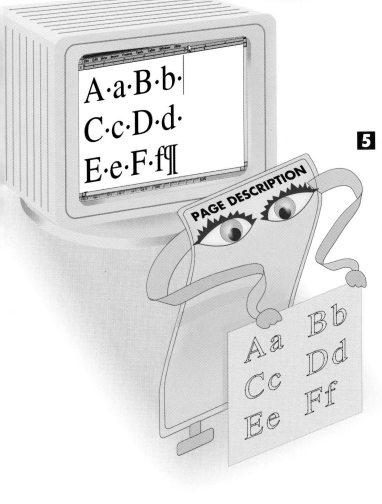

5 The page description language then translates the commands for individual characters into a bitmap for the entire page, and sends the electrical signals that control the placement of dots on paper, one row of dots at a time, to produce that page. Under this scheme, a document's page is seen by the page description language as one large graphic, which may happen to contain text and/or real graphic images.

6

HOW GRAPHICS SOFTWARE WORKS

CONTENTS

WE THINK OF the Mona Lisa as a brilliant example of Renaissance art…as a mysterious image…or as a thoughtful study in composition, light, and shadow. We don't think of it as a mathematical formula.

But in the computer world, all art, graphics, shapes, colors, and lines involve some type of mathematical algorithm. That statement isn't meant to belittle the works of Leonardo and other great artists. Mathematical algorithms cannot create art; that still takes a true artist, whether the artist's tools are brush, oils, and canvas, or a computerized stylus. But math embedded in specific file formats can describe any piece of existing art. A graphics-file image of the Mona Lisa that you can display on your PC is the result of mathematical calculations on the bytes of data saved in that file.

Of course, there was a time when it was absurd to think about displaying the Mona Lisa on a computer screen in a form even remotely resembling the original. The first IBM PCs and their clones were designed primarily to handle text—a much simpler proposition than graphics. Almost begrudgingly, the computer manufacturers offered a graphics adapter to replace the video card that presented only text. The result was a display that was fit for neither words nor pictures. The text was clunky and hard to read. You were limited to showing only four colors at a time from a selection of 16, and the resolution was on a par with a connect-the-dots drawing. You could do a better job of recreating Leonardo's masterpiece with a paint-by-numbers kit than you could with the PCs of the early 80s.

That has changed now for four reasons: the development of computer monitors capable of rendering images with near-photographic resolution; the creation of graphics boards that match the resolution of those monitors; the lowering of memory and hard-drive prices that has made it easier to afford a PC that can store the enormous amounts of data needed to create high-resolution, realistic images; and the continuing growth of processing power that gives PCs the muscle to display and manipulate high-resolution images with acceptable speed.

In tandem with these hardware developments, software manufacturers have created amazing programs for displaying and working with high-quality graphics. Today, all the capabilities of a darkroom and an artist's studio are available on a personal computer. You can retouch, lighten, darken, crop, and do virtually anything else to a computer image that you could to a photograph. You could do more, really—with a PC, even a semiskilled retoucher could make Mona Lisa frown. Other software lets an artist re-create the effects of different media—oils, watercolors, airbrush, charcoal. The artist can even mix media in ways that are difficult to match in real life—to obtain, say, the effect of a water-based paint dissolving crayon lines on paper.

Modern PC graphics are not just about creating pretty pictures. We live in a world of images and colors—not a world of words, which are after all only abstractions for the things we see, feel, touch, and do. We use shape and color in everyday life to convey information faster than words can. Just consider the red, octagonal stop sign; you can be illiterate and know what it means. So, too, in computers, graphics are an increasingly important way of conveying information. Imagine an on-screen map of a city, showing in red those zip code areas where family income is more than $100,000. You comprehend it at a glance. A spreadsheet printout of the same information consisting of nothing but numbers would require ponderous study to comprehend.

Shape and color are information as surely as words are. The difference is that words are nicely defined and limited, but shapes and colors have infinite variations, which means that a PC handling graphics is up against a more daunting job. There are two basic ways that graphics software copes with this infinity of variation: through bitmapped and vector graphics. In the two chapters in this section, we'll examine how bitmapped and vector images are stored, how graphics software translates each into the signals needed to display either type of image on the monitor, and the advantages and disadvantages of each.

How Bitmapped Graphics Work

WHEN YOU READ the Sunday funnies, you're looking at a hardcopy version of one of the two basic ways in which a computer displays graphics. Put a magnifying glass to the color comics and you'll see that they are made up of hundreds of dots of red, blue, and yellow ink. Different colors and shades are created by varying the sizes of the dots. Large red and yellow dots and small blue dots create a shade of orange. Increase the size of the blue dots in the same area, and the color becomes brown.

One important difference between printed color and monitor color is that the monitor uses green dots instead of yellow. Also, printed color is *subtractive*, which means that equal amounts of red, blue, and yellow absorb (subtract) all colors so that no color is reflected, creating black; monitor color is *additive*, meaning that equal amounts of red, blue, and green add all colors of light to produce white. But both methods use three basic colors to produce all the colors you see on paper or on screen.

If you look at a comic strip too closely, all you see are the dots themselves, rather than the image they are creating. But hold the comics away from you, and the dots resolve themselves into a single image.

If you were to study a comic strip and make a meticulous record of the position, size, and color of each dot, you would in effect create a noncomputerized version of one of the most common forms of computer graphics, a bitmap. As its name implies, a bitmap contains a specific map of all the bits of data—location and color information—that make up a computer image by lighting up specific pixels on a monitor. (*Pixel* stands for *picture element*, the smallest area of a monitor's screen that can be turned on or off to help create an image.)

To your eyes, the computer image is the same as a comic strip held at arm's length. You see lines, curves, and shadings. But for the software that displays a bitmap, it's like looking at the comic strip through a magnifying glass. The software is not aware of any lines, shapes, or shadings. It is aware only of individual dots of color. The software doesn't display a line in a bitmap; rather, it displays a collection of colored dots, some of which happen to fall together to create a line here, others of which wind up forming a curve there, and still others of which blend together to create an expanse of a certain color.

Because the software working with bitmaps is unaware of shapes and lines, you can't use the program to simply move or reshape some object in the bitmap. Instead, you must change each of the bits that make up the object. For that reason, bitmaps are useful when an image is relatively static, as Microsoft Windows's icons and wallpapers are. Colors usually can be changed easily within a bitmap, but to easily change the size or shape of objects contained in a bitmapped image, the image first would have to be converted to the other form in which a computer stores graphics: a *vector* image, which we'll explore in the next chapter.

Here, we'll look at how bitmaps are stored on disk, how the files are read by your PC to display the bitmapped image on screen, and how compression techniques are used to compact the vast amounts of information that go into a bitmap.

How Bitmapped Graphics Work

1 When a graphics program reads a bitmapped file, it first finds information contained in the file's header, which is several bytes at the beginning of the file that contain information the program needs to interpret the data in the rest of the file. The header begins with a *signature* that identifies the file as a bitmap. (Windows bitmaps, for example, begin with the letters *BM*.) Following the signature, the header tells the width and height of the image in pixels, and then defines the *palette* (how many and which colors are used in the image).

2 After determining the parameters of the graphic file, the program reads the bytes of data following the header that contain the image as a pattern of bits. The simplest bitmapped image is one that has only black and white pixels. For images of this type, the graphics program needs only two pieces of information: the location of a pixel and whether to turn the pixel on or off. The locations of the pixels are determined by the width and height of the image as defined in the header. In the crude image of a man in a hat, the line pixels wrap every 11 bits to the next row of pixels.

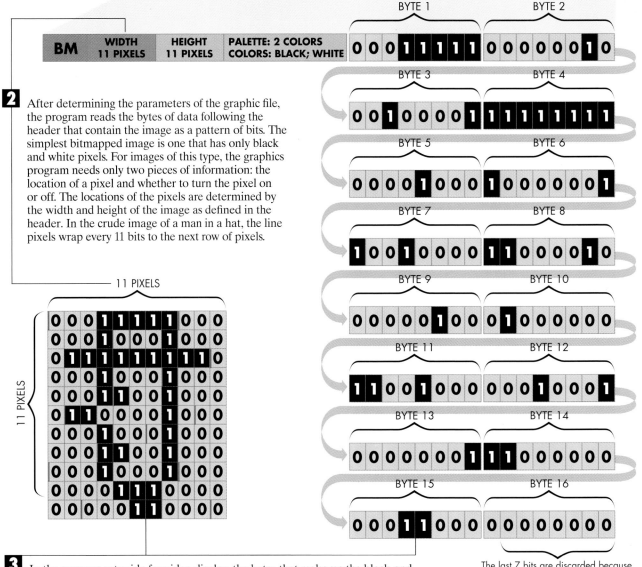

3 In the memory set aside for video display, the bytes that make up the black-and-white image consist of some bits set to 1, meaning that a pixel that corresponds to that bit should be turned on, and other bits set to 0 to indicate that their matching pixels should be turned off. The man in the hat consists of 121 pixels, which in a black-and-white image can be stored in 16 bytes.

The last 7 bits are discarded because they fall outside the matrix of pixels set up in the header.

BM | WIDTH | HEIGHT | PALETTE | COLOR | RED | GREEN | BLUE | HEX BYTE VALUE
1h 2h 3h 4h 5h 6h 7h 8h 9h 10h

4 A color bitmap requires more than 1 bit per pixel. Eight bits (or 1 byte) per pixel is enough data to define a palette of 256 colors because 8 bits of binary information can have a total of 256 possible values (2^8). Each of the possible 8-bit values is matched in the palette to a specific combination of red, blue, and green dots that make up a single pixel. (Although the dots of color are separate from each other, they're close enough together that the eye sees them as a single point of blended color.)

BM | WIDTH | HEIGHT | RED | GREEN | BLUE | HEX BYTE VALUE | COLOR VALUE
1h 2h 3h 4h 5h 6h 7h 8h 9h 10h

5 For 24-bit graphics, 3 bytes of memory are used to define each pixel. Three bytes provide enough data to define more than 16 million possible colors (2^{24}), which is why 24-bit color is sometimes referred to as *true color*—it's difficult to image that any real-life shade would not be among the 16 million. A common way of rendering 24-bit color is to have each of the three bytes assigned to a pixel represent the amount of red, green, or blue that make up the pixel. The values of the three bytes determine how much of each color goes into the pixel. Think of the difference between 8-bit and 24-bit color this way: 8-bit lets you choose from 256 colors that are "premixed," the way some cans of house paint are sold; a 24-bit method essentially mixes custom colors for each pixel on the fly. [*Continued on next page.*]

How Bitmapped Graphics Work

VIDEO RAM

40Eh 25h E02h 3h

6 Regardless of the method used, after interpreting the bitmap file, the graphics software puts the values for the pixels in the memory used by the video adapter. The adapter, in turn, uses that data in memory to send the electronic signals that set the intensity of each of the dots of red, green, and blue that make up the pixel.

7 The monitor responds to the video card's signals by sending electron streams of varying intensities to different phosphors—one phosphor for each of the three colors—painted on the inside of the monitor's screen. The phosphors glow brighter or dimmer, depending on the intensity of the electron stream that energizes them.

8 Because bitmap files can get extremely big, some image file formats have built-in compression, called *run-length encoding* (RLE), that compresses the data in the files to take up less room on disk. RLE takes advantage of the fact that, in many images, large stretches of pixels are exactly the same. RLE works by using something called a *key byte,* which tells the software if the next byte represents several pixels or only one. The software checks the first bit of the key byte. If it's a 1, the software reads the value of the remaining 7 bits in the byte—we'll call the value *N*—and interprets the values of the next *N* bytes as color combinations for individual, consecutive pixels. At the end of the *N* bytes, there is another key byte.

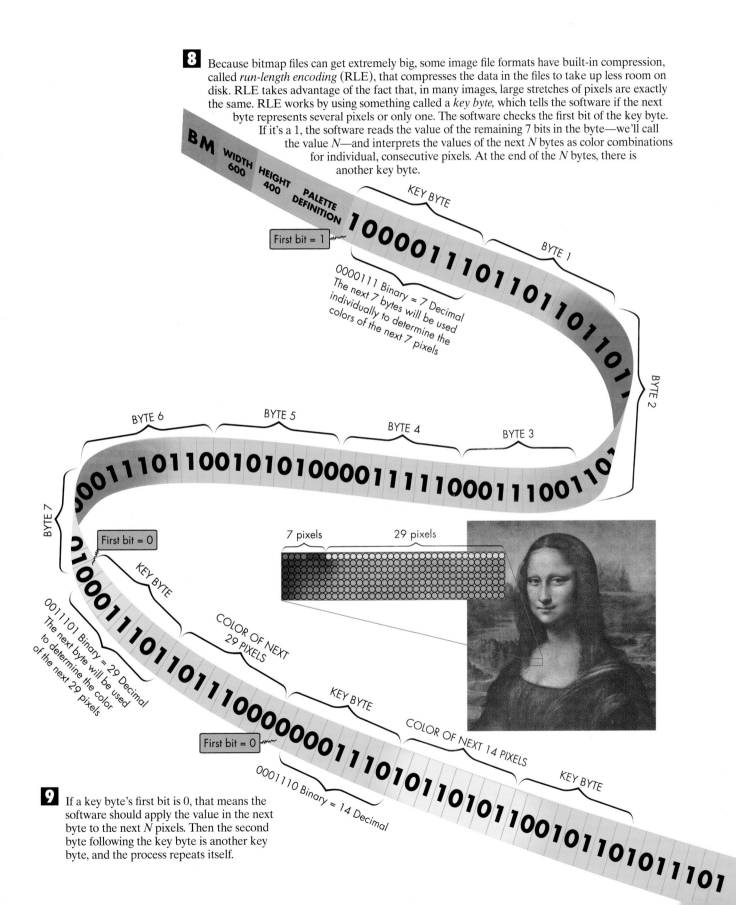

First bit = 1

0000111 Binary = 7 Decimal
The next 7 bytes will be used individually to determine the colors of the next 7 pixels

KEY BYTE

BYTE 1

BYTE 2

BYTE 6 BYTE 5 BYTE 4 BYTE 3

BYTE 7

First bit = 0

KEY BYTE

0011101 Binary = 29 Decimal
The next byte will be used to determine the color of the next 29 pixels

COLOR OF NEXT 29 PIXELS

KEY BYTE

COLOR OF NEXT 14 PIXELS

First bit = 0

0001110 Binary = 14 Decimal

KEY BYTE

7 pixels   29 pixels

BM WIDTH 600 HEIGHT 400 PALETTE DEFINITION

9 If a key byte's first bit is 0, that means the software should apply the value in the next byte to the next *N* pixels. Then the second byte following the key byte is another key byte, and the process repeats itself.

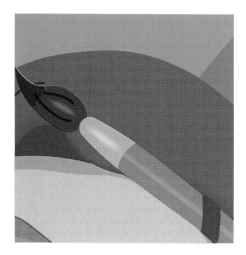

How Vector Graphics Work

F A COMIC strip is a hardcopy analogy for a bitmapped graphic, then an architect's blueprint is the hardcopy parallel to the *vector* graphic, the other common form of computer image.

A blueprint doesn't show the placement of each brick and board that goes into a building. Rather, the construction team—the human equivalent of the graphics software—uses the blueprint as a guide to the overall features of the building and figures out where to put individual bricks and boards.

Similarly, a vector graphic doesn't store the data about where individual pixels are displayed or what color they should be, as does a bitmapped graphic. Instead, the vector graphic stores a mathematical formula that describes the shapes and colors that make up the image—a sort of blueprint for the graphic.

A blueprint has a scale that tells how many feet are represented by each inch on the drawing. The scale is a variable; by changing only the value of the scale, the plans for a manor can become plans for a doll house. Similarly, a vector-graphic formula includes variables that can be changed to manipulate the size, shapes, or colors of the image. When you manipulate the image on screen with a mouse and with the coloring and drawing tools provided by the software, the program quietly converts your actions into the numbers the formula needs. When the graphics program executes the formula, the program inserts the values you've given it and builds the image.

Today, many blueprints are *literally* vector graphics. *Computer-aided design* (CAD) programs let architects and engineers do their drawings on screen. The CAD program saves a mathematical three-dimensional model of the plans; with negligible effort, the CAD user can rotate the drawing to look at it from different angles or strip away layers to look at parts of the plans hidden beneath. To do something even remotely similar with bitmapped graphics would require individual drawings for each view of the object.

Vector graphics are not limited to CAD programs. You've used vector graphics if you've played certain games. (Not all games use vector graphics; some scroll through a large bitmap or rapidly substitute a series of bitmaps to produce animation.) Outline typefaces are a form of vector graphic (see

Chapter 14). A common example of a vector image is the graph produced by an electronic spreadsheet. If you change the numbers used to create a bar graph, the vector formulas for the graph use the new information to change the size of the bars.

We'll look here at how vector graphics are stored, modified, and displayed.

How Vector Graphics Work

1 A vector-based graphic image is stored in a file as a *display list* that describes in mathematical terms every shape, or object, in the image along with its location and properties, such as line width and *fill* (the color or pattern that fills a shape). The display list also specifies the hierarchy of objects—which ones should be drawn first and which are on top of others.

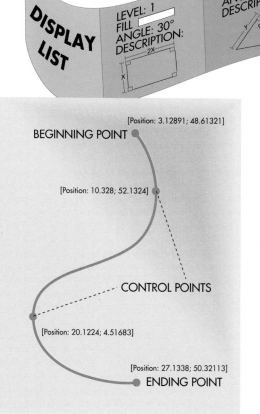

DISPLAY LIST

LEVEL: 1
FILL
ANGLE: 30°
DESCRIPTION:

LEVEL: 1
FILL
ANGLE: 60°
DESCRIPTION:

LEVEL: 1
FILL
ANGLE: 90°
DESCRIPTION:

2 To draw an object, the program needs to know the locations of only a few points. The formula for a Bezier curve, for example, needs only four points: the beginning point, the ending point, and two control points that determine how far the curve is "pulled" away from a straight line.

[Position: 3.12891; 48.61321]
BEGINNING POINT

[Position: 10.328; 52.1324]

CONTROL POINTS

[Position: 20.1224; 4.51683]

[Position: 27.1338; 50.32113]
ENDING POINT

3 The points are each defined by two numbers—one for the point's vertical position and the other for the horizontal position. Each of those numbers is stored to a much higher degree of precision than could be specified by the pixel locations alone. This precision allows the software to draw the curve accurately, no matter how much its size is increased or decreased, or the curve is moved or otherwise manipulated.

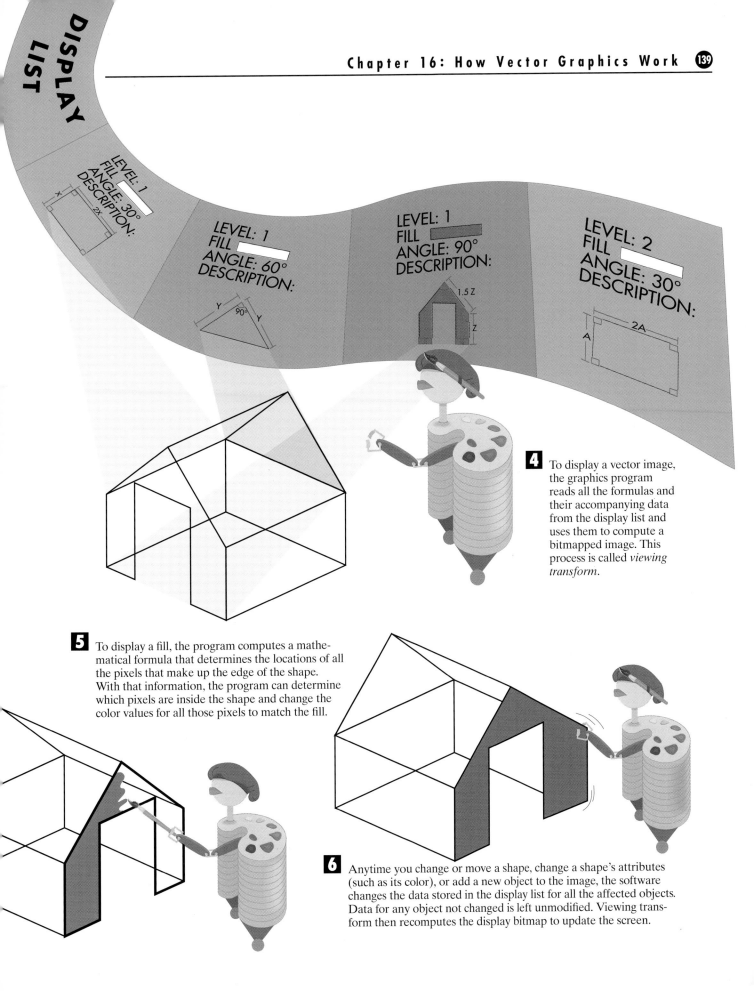

DISPLAY LIST

LEVEL: 1
FILL
ANGLE: 30°
DESCRIPTION:

LEVEL: 1
FILL
ANGLE: 60°
DESCRIPTION:

LEVEL: 1
FILL
ANGLE: 90°
DESCRIPTION:

LEVEL: 2
FILL
ANGLE: 30°
DESCRIPTION:

4 To display a vector image, the graphics program reads all the formulas and their accompanying data from the display list and uses them to compute a bitmapped image. This process is called *viewing transform*.

5 To display a fill, the program computes a mathematical formula that determines the locations of all the pixels that make up the edge of the shape. With that information, the program can determine which pixels are inside the shape and change the color values for all those pixels to match the fill.

6 Anytime you change or move a shape, change a shape's attributes (such as its color), or add a new object to the image, the software changes the data stored in the display list for all the affected objects. Data for any object not changed is left unmodified. Viewing transform then recomputes the display bitmap to update the screen.

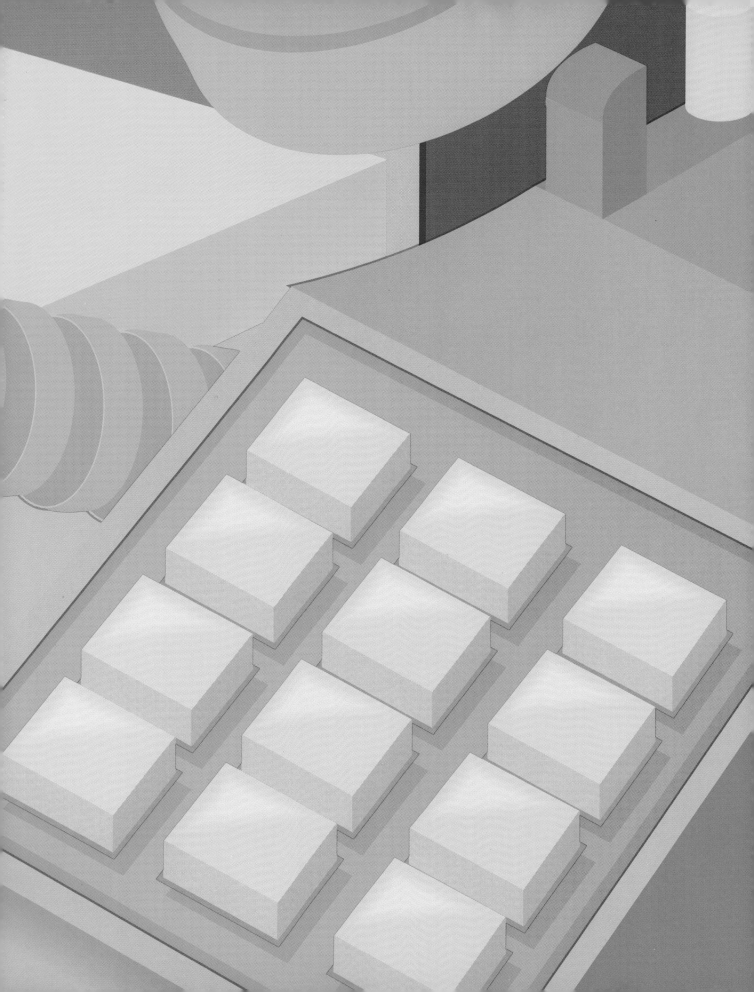

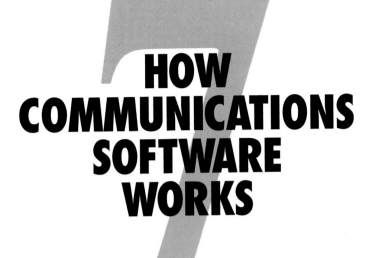

HOW COMMUNICATIONS SOFTWARE WORKS

CONTENTS

OVERVIEW

WORKING WITH A personal computer can be a lonely affair. Most of the time it's just you and the machine. If you're not careful, you'll find you've become a recluse, entranced by all the wonderful things you've learned to do with your PC and oblivious to the real world. Computing is seductive. It bestows new powers and just waits to do your bidding. But in return, your PC asks that you spend long hours stroking its keys, caressing its mouse. *Beep*—it's just you and me, master.

There is a cure for the loneliness, and it's available through the computer itself. The fix is a modem and telecommunications software. Together, they transform the PC from a solitary fetish into an open door leading to a new world of people, knowledge, and ideas. Even if you work in a mountain cabin, the rest of the world is just a few keystrokes away in the forms of giant systems of data and electronic mail, such as CompuServe, and modest, local electronic bulletin-board systems run by hobbyists. These allow you to make close friends you may never see in person, access expert advice you couldn't buy, and tap into founts of data that used to be the private purview of big business and information brokers.

All this is possible through an unlikely combination of technologies. Conventional telephone lines are not designed to handle computer data, especially at the speed at which computers can generate that information. Phone lines are designed for a more leisurely mode of data transmission—the human voice. The word *Hello* takes about one second to say; during that time, a modern modem can transmit the entire text of the page that you're reading now. But the modem must do some fast and fancy tricks with that data before it can send it across the telephone lines. That's because phone lines are designed for *analog* signals, which vary a continuous electrical signal to capture the constantly changing pitch and volume of spoken words. PCs can send data only in *digital* form, as a series of 0s and 1s. The modem is the translator between the two types of signals, and your telecommunications software is the referee that makes sure modems on both ends of a connection are using the same rules.

In this section, we'll look at how communications software works with the modem to send digital information as analog signals and how *data transfer protocols* ensure the accuracy of data sent over modem lines.

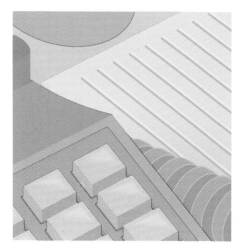

CHAPTER
17

How Communications Software Operates a Modem

UNLIKE MOST SOFTWARE that's designed to let you manipulate data stored as documents, spreadsheets, or databases on your hard drive, communications programs do very little permanent changing of data. When you download a file from CompuServe or Prodigy, communications software lets you save the file to disk, and many communications programs have built-in editors that let you write messages you can zap across the phone lines as electronic mail, or e-mail. But generally, communications software juggles its data on the fly, acting more like a traffic cop than like a builder of highways.

The main function of communications software is to oversee the rapid ushering of data in and out of your PC through one of the COM ports. When the software does its job well, it becomes *transparent*—you aren't aware that you're using some particular software. Instead, you are free to concentrate your attention on the stream of messages that appear magically on your screen from far-off places and from people you've never met. You become conscious of your communications program only when it fails to do its job properly and those streams of messages turn into electronic garbage: "The real point of the argument is #####ljj da kj**;' kjdllkj;s sl!!!"

The reason such glitches happen is that the truce between the digital data of 0s and 1s that your computer uses and the analog signals into which your modem must translate those 0s and 1s is fragile. If you've ever seen the wavy line on an oscilloscope as it tracks the sounds of someone's voice or the beat of a heart, you've looked at a visual representation of analog data—a steady line of widely varying values that are represented by the varying height of the line. Digital signals, though, do not vary; they are either on or off. On an oscilloscope, a 0 bit would be a flat line at the bottom of the screen; a 1 bit would be a flat line at the top of the screen.

At the very simplest level, it's not hard to make a telephone analog signal represent 0s and 1s. All the software and modem must do is send a low-pitched sound across the phone line to stand for a 0 and a high-pitched sound to represent a 1. This is called *modulation*; the reverse process on the other end of the phone line is called *demodulation*. A combination of the first syllables of these terms is the source of the word *modem*.

The trouble with this method, however, is that phone lines are not capable of changing pitch faster than about 600 times a second, which would represent only 600 bits each second. Allowing for the overhead time that communications programs add for error checking, 600 bits a second translates to fewer than 10 words a second under ideal conditions. Of course, conditions are never ideal, and the result is that 600 bits a second is much too slow. Most of us can read faster than the text can appear on screen, and especially if you're on a long-distance connection, you want to make every second count. The trick is to pack more information—more bits—into each pitch change by making different analog pitches represent specific combinations of multiple 0s and 1s. There are two methods for doing this.

One method is *group coding,* which lets different analog frequencies stand for different combinations of bits. For example, to send data at 1,200 bits per second, the two modems use four different frequencies to represent the four possible combinations of two bits: 00, 01, 10, and 11.

The other method used for increasing data transmission speeds is on-the-fly data compression, in which software built into the modems looks for patterns that are repeated in the data and substitutes a form of shorthand that is recognized and translated back into the original data by the receiving modem.

The refereeing job that communications programs must do is also important. If all computer systems were identical, there'd be no need for this refereeing. But they're not. Each system that acts as a *host*—that is, allows your PC to dial into it—can choose from among about 120 combinations of rules for how data is grouped, how each computer lets the other know it's ready to send data, and how to do elementary error checking. As the traffic cop for the remote system, it's your communications software's job to bundle your data into properly formatted *data packets* for the host system and to make sure your PC is using the same rules as the host is.

Data bits, parity bits, and start/stop bits are signposts that identify the type of data packet the software is using. A data packet is a single collection of bits that encodes a single alphanumeric character. Without the bit signposts, a system receiving data would have no way of knowing when a stream of bits stops representing one character and begins representing another character.

The vagaries inherent in sending the same data by so many methods can at times make setting up a communications program frustrating. You can rarely just install the program on your hard drive, run it, and then start using it. You must know how a host system expects to receive and send data, and you must match settings on the software to those of each host you use. New software is appearing that handles all this automatically by trying each setting until it finds one that works. But in the meantime, you can take comfort in the fact that once you have a communications program set up properly, you rarely have to be concerned with the setup again. Once that's done, the communications software melts away the barriers of distance, and the world is at your fingertips.

How Software Communicates with a Host System

1 When you load your communications software, it sends a signal (usually about 5 volts of electricity) along a specific wire that is one of many making up the cable leading from your COM port to your modem. (If you have an internal modem, the procedure is the same, except that the signals are sent to the modem-board pins that plug into an expansion slot.) This signal, called a *Data Terminal Ready* (DTR), tells the modem that your PC is turned on and ready to send data. The modem, in turn, sends a signal along a different wire to let your software know that it's turned on and ready to receive data. Its signal is called a *Data Set Ready* (DSR).

DTR

DSR

MR TR OH HS CD SD RD AA

AT & K3X4EOUl

MR TR OH HS CD SD RD AA

2 Your software communicates with your modem by using a standard set of commands that the modem is designed to recognize. Usually, this is a language called the *Hayes AT command set,* named after the Hayes modems that popularized the commands and the most frequently used command, AT, which is used to get the modem's **AT**tention. When you select a communications host from your software's menu, the software sends a set of *initialization commands.* These commands make sure that the modem is set to the proper defaults.

3 The software then sends a signal along another specific wire leading to the modem, telling the modem to go *off hook*—the same as if you were picking up the handset from a telephone. It follows that with a command to dial the phone, followed by the phone number to use. For example, the command ATDT18009679600 translates as "Attention Dial Tone" followed by the 800 phone number for MCI Mail. When the host answers the call, the two modems send each other various tones to identify themselves.

CARRIER SIGNAL

4 When the connection to the host system is made, the modem sends your communications software a *Carrier Detect* (CD) signal. This tells the software the modem is receiving a *carrier signal*, a steady tone of a certain frequency that the software and modem will *modulate*, or modify, to represent digital data. If, during any of these first actions, the modem does not receive the type of signal it's supposed to, it will notify the software, which will then display an error message on your screen. [*Continued on next page.*]

How Software Communicates with a Host System

5 Before any real data can be exchanged, your software and the host perform a process called a *handshake*, in which the two systems introduce themselves to each other to make sure they're using the same strategy for sending and receiving data. The two systems must agree on *transmission speed, flow control, data bits, start/stop bits, parity,* and *duplex*.

* **Transmission speed** is mostly negotiated by the modem. High-speed transmissions use two methods—group coding or on-the-fly data compression—to overcome the limits at which phone signals can be modulated. In the example of group coding shown at the right, the modem would send tones at frequencies 2, 4, 2, 1, 3, 3, 4 to send the binary sequence of 01 11 01 00 10 10 11.

* **Flow control** regulates the sending and receiving of information at the serial port so that a receiving computer is not overrun with data while it is busy with another task, such as routing data to a disk or printer. Using *XON/XOFF* flow control, software on the receiving end sends a ^S (the same signal generated by pressing Ctrl-S) to halt the flow of data, and a ^Q (Ctrl-Q) to turn it back on. The other method relies on the modems to send RTS/CTS (Request to Send/ Clear to Send) signals to each other. The two systems may use either, none, or both of the methods.

* **Data bits** must be set properly because although most systems use 8 bits to represent alphanumeric characters, some use 7. Both systems must use the same scheme.

* **Parity bits** are used for rudimentary error checking. Depending on what scheme the two systems use—even, odd, none, or some specialized method—both systems add up the bits contained in the data packet and add another bit, called the parity bit. It may be either a 0 bit or a 1 bit, depending on which is needed to make the total either an even number or an odd number. Whether the number should be even or odd depends on the method the systems are using. If the result is odd when it should be even—or vice versa—the software knows something is wrong with the data in the packet. Not all systems use parity bits.

		1	2	3	4
FREQUENCY					
BIT COMBINATIONS		**00**	**01**	**10**	**11**

01 11 01 00 10 10 11

DATA PACKET

1	0 0 1 0 1 1 1 0	1	0

START BIT — DATA BITS — PARITY BIT — STOP BIT

* **Start/stop bits** are used to signal the start and end of a data packet. The beginning of a packet is always signaled by 1 bit, but systems may use either 1 or 2 bits to signal the end of a packet. Both systems must use the same number of stop bits.

* **Full-duplex and half-duplex** refer to which system, the host or the remote, is responsible for displaying text on the remote PC screen. In this instance, the two systems should *not* be assigned to the same settings—one must be half-duplex and one must be full-duplex. If both are full-duplex, all characters sent between the systems will appear twice. If both are half-duplex, nothing will appear on the remote screen. Duplex settings are sometimes referred to as *echo on/off*.

6 If any of the settings used by your software do not complement the setting of the host, no connection will be established or the connection will produce an unintelligible string of gibberish. But if the two systems complete the handshaking properly, your communications software sends a *Request to Send* (RTS) signal over a specific wire to the modem. This signal asks the modem if it's ready to receive data from the PC. Unless the modem is too busy handling other data, it sends a *Clear to Send* (CTS) signal back to the software over a separate wire. If your modem gets overloaded with more data than it can handle, it will drop the CTS signal and your software will wait to send more data.

RTS

CTS

7 Most host systems require you to *log on*; that is, identify yourself with a name and password. While the password is being typed in, duplex is usually turned off so that your password will not display on screen. Usually, communications software has a *learn* feature that observes the keystrokes you use to log on and records them to disk. The information in the file can then be used in future sessions to log on to the same host automatically.

MR TR OH HS CD SD RD AA

BYE

CD

8 When you give your software the command to end a communications session, the software sends an ATH command to tell the modem to hang up. If the host ends the connection first, the modem stops sending a voltage along the wire used for a Carrier Detect (CD) signal, and your software will notify you that the carrier has been lost.

MR TR OH HS CD SD RD AA

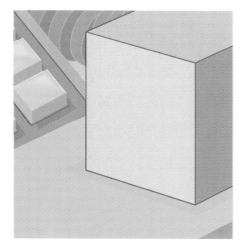

CHAPTER
18

How Data Transfer Protocols Work

ALL TELEPHONE LINES are, to some extent, "dirty." That's not a reference to those infamous 900 numbers. It's a slang expression that describes the various ways that stray electrical signals, other telephone transmissions, and even sunspots can corrupt a telephone-line signal. Such disruptions are not always serious, but when a communications session encounters extreme dirt on the phone line, some of the bits in the data being transmitted are dropped, added to, or changed.

Ordinarily, if you're working with plain-text files or just typing messages while you're on line, dirty transmissions are no problem unless the connection is so bad that one of the modems interprets some stray interference as a command to log off. But if all that happens is that you get a message in which interference changes a few letters, you can still figure out what the message's author intended. (In fact, errors are more likely to be typos and misspellings than dirt-induced.)

But suppose you're downloading a neat new shareware program from a bulletin board? Or you're sending a spreadsheet with next year's annual budget? In the first instance, changing just one bit in the file could render the program inoperable. However, if the program didn't work, you simply wouldn't use it, and all you'd lose would be some downloading time. But the second example could result in a more insidious error because the spreadsheet could appear fine, although one number in it had changed. If you'd budgeted, say, $1,000 for the office coffee machine, changing only one particular bit would turn the figure into $9,000. Or worse still for the caffeine addicts in your office, changing just one other bit would convert the number to $0,000. The spreadsheet would continue to function normally, and the change would be so subtle you might never spot it.

To avoid such errors, all communications programs and host systems provide *data transfer protocols* for transferring *binary* (non-text) files. These are schemes in which a system sending data also provides the receiving system with enough information so the second system can verify that the data it receives is identical to the data the first system sent.

There are dozens of such protocols, the best known of which are *Xmodem, Zmodem, Ymodem,* and *Kermit*. Many of these have variations that improve the speed of transfers or allow your software to modify its operations to cope with varying degrees of dirt on phone lines. These protocols are some of the best examples of the altruism you sometimes find in the computer world. Most of these schemes were developed by individuals who sought their own solutions to the problem of garbled transmissions and who then put those fixes into the public domain. Now, any software developer can incorporate these protocols into their own communications programs. The result has been standards that are used widely throughout the computer communications world. It is virtually impossible for you to use any communications program that doesn't provide at least one transfer protocol suitable for use with any host system to which you connect.

Each of the protocols varies somewhat in its efficiency and features. With some, for example, if a phone line is so garbled that you lose the connection in the middle of downloading a file, the protocol will let you try again and continue downloading where the transmission left off rather than forcing you to download the entire file again. Generally, however, the principles behind each of the protocols are similar. We'll look here at an Xmodem transfer, one of the most commonly used protocols.

How an Xmodem File Transfer Works

1 During an Xmodem file transfer, the sending system breaks the file up into separate blocks, usually of 128 bytes each. To each block, the protocol adds a header consisting of the hexadecimal number 01, followed by 2 bytes that contain the block number. (Some variations of many protocols allow you to send larger blocks over lines that you believe to be relatively clean, or smaller blocks on lines that may be dirty and often require the blocks to be retransmitted.)

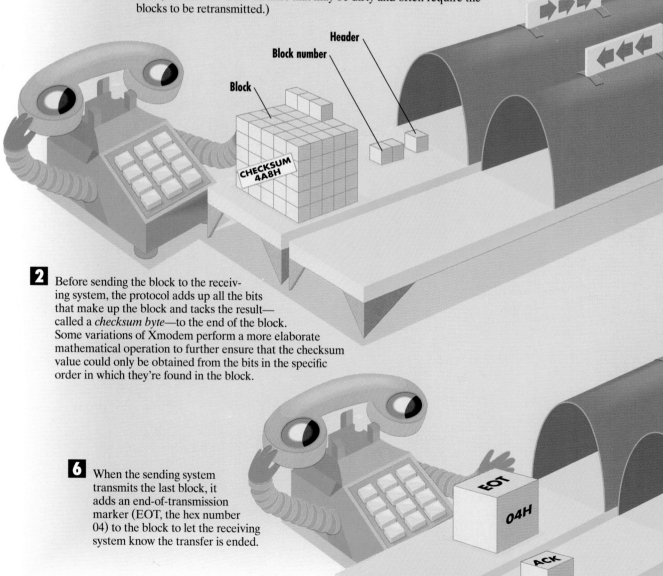

Header

Block number

Block

CHECKSUM 4A8H

2 Before sending the block to the receiving system, the protocol adds up all the bits that make up the block and tacks the result— called a *checksum byte*—to the end of the block. Some variations of Xmodem perform a more elaborate mathematical operation to further ensure that the checksum value could only be obtained from the bits in the specific order in which they're found in the block.

6 When the sending system transmits the last block, it adds an end-of-transmission marker (EOT, the hex number 04) to the block to let the receiving system know the transfer is ended.

EOT 04H

ACK

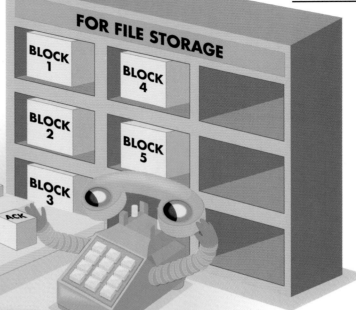

3 When the communications software at the receiving system gets the block, it checks to make sure the block is in the proper sequence. It then performs the same mathematical operation on the bits that the sending system performed and checks its results against the result contained in the checksum byte sent with the block.

4 If the two checksums are identical, the software adds the block to the file being saved on disk and sends the number 06 hex, which is an *acknowledgment signal* (ACK). The ACK tells the sending system that everything in the block checked out and that it should send the next block.

5 If a block is sent out of sequence or if line noise has changed the values in the block so that the receiving software's checksum calculation doesn't match the checksum sent with the block, the software discards the block. It then sends the first system the number 15 hex, which is called a *negative acknowledgment signal,* or *NAK*. This tells the sending system that something was wrong with the block and that it should be sent again. This process is repeated until the block arrives intact or until the routine has failed several times in a row. The latter case indicates that the phone connection is so dirty that the completion of a successful transfer is unlikely. Usually, the software will then terminate the transfer. In such a situation, the best thing for the person on the receiving end to do is break the connection and call the host again, hoping for a cleaner connection.

HOW WINDOWS WORKS

CONTENTS

FOR THOSE WHO'VE been with the personal computer revolution since its inception, all the graphic buttons, scroll bars, drop-down menus, pointers, and hourglasses may at first appear busy, even confusing. But they all form a seductive method for using software. The more you use Windows programs, the more it seems as if this were the way PCs were meant to be used. Before long, reaching for the mouse is as natural as picking up a pencil.

But Windows has altered more than the face of personal computer software. Behind the push-button graphic interface, the soul of software has changed. The appearance of Windows affects how you use software, but what's going on beneath the surface changes what you can do with software.

Windows is more than a look. It's a way of creating software—an approach that reaches beyond an individual program to shape the fundamental ways in which software and hardware resources are used and code and data are shared. If you use only one Windows program, the advantages of Windows are not apparent. In fact, compared to the DOS text-based version of the same software, a Windows program is likely to be slower and demand more powerful processors and larger memory and disk storage. But once you start using two Windows programs, Windows begins to make sense. Use still more Windows programs, and its way of working quickly becomes indispensable.

The skills you learn with one Windows program are easily transferred to other Windows programs. But even more important, the distinction between one program and another begins to fade. Your word-processor document may have a worksheet created by a spreadsheet program and an illustration created by still another program. Through the process of *object linking and embedding* (OLE), double-clicking on the icon that represents a worksheet or illustration takes you to the programs that created those objects. You have, in effect, a super-software application that lets you build on the combined strengths of the three individual programs. The whole becomes more than the sum of its parts.

What makes all this possible is the modularity of Windows. Different software written by different programmers can use the same functions built into the Windows environment. This isn't simply a matter of making programmers' jobs easier; it ensures consistency and interaction among applications, which benefits the user.

Windows is not the only integrated graphic interface. OS/2 and the Macintosh provide similar benefits. But the last few years have seen a consistent move by software developers and users toward Windows. The argument about which is the best graphic environment has already been won, not by the superiority of one technical subtlety over another, but by the force of the marketplace. PC users are voting with their dollars by buying millions of Windows programs. It is the face and soul of all computing to come.

In this section, we'll look at the modularity and other inner workings of Windows to explain how it provides its primary benefits—the easy-to-use graphic interface, the ability to multitask several applications at the same time, and the sharing of data and program code. Like many other systems, the simpler it appears on the surface, the more complex— and fascinating—it is beneath.

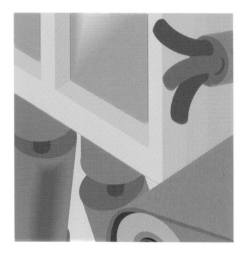

How Windows's Graphic Interface Works

THE WORD MOST often used to describe the graphic interface used by Windows is "intuitive." But the interface is not really intuitive—at least not for humans. Trained chimps and chickens work by pointing at graphic images; humans work through the medium of words.

Is using Windows easier than typing words at a DOS C: prompt? Sure it is. But it's not just the graphic nature of Windows that makes it easier. In fact, the more graphic the interface becomes, the more difficult it is to use. A case in point is just about any of the graphics-only icons found on the tool-bar buttons of many Windows applications. The artists who create these icons strain the human imagination in their attempts to use images to communicate ideas that are instantly understood in words. For example, the icon for the thesaurus feature of a certain word processor is an image of an open book. There are dozens of associations that a user might make with an open book before stumbling across "thesaurus."

The truth is that the graphic interface of Windows succeeds because it provides a better way of working with words, not images. The most often-used feature of the Windows interface is the strip of menus at the top of the screen. The choices with which they are laden are easy to understand because they're based on words. The secret of Windows's interface is not so much its graphic nature as the fact that it presents you with all the information you need to use a program. You may still be using words, but you are presented with lists from which to make your choices. You don't have to memorize all those words, as you would to work from a DOS prompt.

But the graphic interface also justifies itself graphically in one way—by providing on-screen tools that emulate those found in the real world. Not all the purely graphic choices are as obscure as the symbol of an open book for a thesaurus. For example, the ruler on a word-processing screen is more natural to use than is typing margin measurements into a form, because margins are, themselves, a visual element. Also, the scroll bars on the side and bottom of a Windows screen *are* actually pretty intuitive. Programs that use visual metaphors of pages, section tabs, and book spines succeed because the graphics have real-world counterparts.

The graphic interface also pays off in the way that you make choices—whether words from a menu or icons from a tool bar. The interface solves the one problem that plagues most computer users—we aren't very good typists. How many times have you tried to do something at a DOS prompt only to have the PC reply, "Bad command or filename"? The mouse's point-and-click features absolve us of all our typing sins.

Point-and-click technology also requires Windows to do an extraordinary amount of work to keep track of what buttons, menu selections, text, or other objects occupy which areas of the screen. Windows must track the location of the insertion point and the mouse's pointer constantly; each time you click a mouse button, Windows also has to know what to do, based on the location of the pointer.

In this chapter, we'll look at how Windows manages its graphic interface and translates movements and clicks on the screen into software functions.

How Windows Manages Its Graphic Interface

1 When a Windows application is launched, it tells Windows what menus it wants displayed; what choices should appear on each menu; and what elements, such as titles, radio buttons, and file-name specs, should appear in dialog boxes.

2 One of the program modules that make up Windows, USER.EXE, draws menus on the screen. If the dialog box requested by the application is not one of the standard designs provided by Windows, USER.EXE creates the box on the fly, following the specs provided by the application. USER.EXE also handles any moving or resizing of windows, dialog boxes, or other elements of the on-screen interface.

3 If different applications ask Windows to draw screen elements that overlap, USER.EXE decides which elements should be on top, based on which application is active in the foreground.

4 To create specific dialog boxes—Color, Font, Open, Save As, Print, Print Setup, Find, and Replace—either USER.EXE or an application directly accesses procedures contained in the *dynamic link library* (DLL) file COMMDLG.DLL, which is the common dialog box DLL. The Windows application might not use COMMDLG, but if it does, then the dialog boxes created by it will look and act exactly like those created by other applications using COMMDLG.DLL. If it uses COMMDLG.DLL, an application only has to make a single function call to COMMDLG—for example, "Create a Save As dialog box"—rather than use many lines of code filled with detailed descriptions of the box. An application also can substitute alternative dialog box designs contained in its own DLL files. (See Chapter 21 for more information on dynamic link libraries.)

USER.EXE

GDI.EXE

5 USER.EXE is concerned only with the Windows interface elements. You can conveniently think of it as handling only those elements—menus, scroll bars, and so on—that *surround* the document, spreadsheet, database form, or whatever other elements make up the data your application is working with. To display the data itself, Windows uses another program module, *GDI.EXE* (Graphics Device Interface). Whenever you type text or numbers or draw with your mouse, those actions are passed to GDI.EXE. You can think of GDI.EXE as handling all the *contents* of an application that are surrounded by the screen elements USER.EXE handles.

6 GDI.EXE inspects the data you've input and any style attributes that it contains, such as boldfaced text or colors. GDI.EXE translates the input from its raw form into a graphic form by rasterizing it. *Rasterizing* translates the text, fonts, and graphic data into the pattern of pixels that must be turned on to represent the data on the screen. GDI.EXE passes this information to the display driver, which actually controls the screen.

7 Any bitmapped image that is to be displayed in the contents area of a Windows screen is handled by GDI.EXE. If you move or resize the bitmap, GDI.EXE instructs the display driver to turn off the pixels that made up the previous version of the bitmap, calculates which new pixels need to be used to create the new version of the bitmap, and sends that information to the display driver, which makes the changes in display memory. This process is called *bitblt* (bit block transfer).

8 If you tell your application to print the text that is on the screen, the application hands the request to GDI.EXE, which sends a rasterized version of the data to the printer driver. In turn, the printer driver provides the printer with the data and commands the printer needs to produce the hard copy.

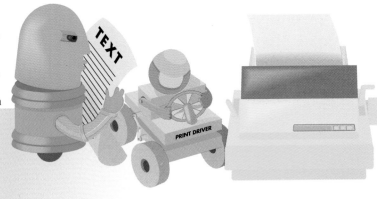

How Windows Handles System Events

1 As you use your applications, Windows constantly monitors your system for interrupts. (See Chapter 3 for more information on interrupts.) These interrupts can be generated by keystrokes, mouse movements or clicks, by an event within an application, or by other hardware events, such as a tick of the internal clock. At the same time, the Windows display driver is watching for interrupts, particularly those from the mouse, which it uses to update the position of the on-screen pointer.

2 When Windows receives an interrupt, it places a message in the *system message queue,* a section of memory reserved for maintaining detailed information about interrupt events—the location of the mouse, the time, keystrokes, and so forth. Windows translates input from any devices—different kinds of mice, for instance—into generic, device-independent messages that any application can read.

3 From the system message queue, Windows routes messages into *application message queues.* Each running application has its own queue. A function called *WinMain*—a part of every Windows application—periodically issues a command called *GetMessage,* which picks up any messages left in the application queue. When GetMessage finds a message in the queue, the application inspects it and performs the appropriate function (which may, in turn, require that it call on services provided by Windows).

4 The application also uses the application queue to send messages to Windows and even to other procedures within the same application. For instance, when you type the letter *A* and after Windows has handled the interrupt through the system queue and application queue, the application places in the application queue a request to display the character on the screen. GDI.EXE retrieves and carries out the request.

5 If an interrupt is a mouse click, Windows must inspect the current position of the mouse pointer and compare that with a map of the screen. Based on what Windows finds at the pointer's position on the map, Windows places a command in the application queue, telling it to carry out a specific procedure. For example, clicking on an Open File icon causes Windows to notify the application through the queue that the user has asked for a File Open procedure.

6 The application places its own message in the application queue to tell Windows to draw the Open File dialog box by using USER.EXE and the routines in COMMDLG.DLL or by using the application's own custom dialog design.

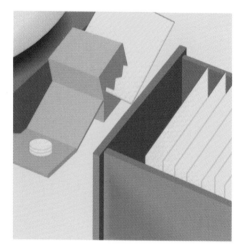

C H A P T E R

20

How Windows Runs Multiple Sessions

FOR MANY WINDOWS users, the primary advantage of Windows is its ability to run several applications simultaneously. Without having to exit a program, you can work in one application, easily pop into another, and then jump back to the first program, picking up right where you left off. Better still, while you're working in the foreground in one program, one or more other applications can be churning away, unseen, in the background, sorting a database, downloading a file, or performing any other lengthy operation that otherwise would monopolize your PC and leave you staring at the screen, unable to get any other work done.

This ability to run several programs at the same time and to zip from one to the other is called *multitasking*, and it reflects the way we all work. Your workday is filled with constant interruptions—phone calls, drop-in visits, sudden inspirations—all events that demand your immediate attention. You have to multitask—why expect less from the software you use?

To multitask, Windows takes advantage of a feature called *protected mode,* which first appeared in the Intel 80286 microprocessor but achieved really workable status only in the Intel 80386 microprocessor and its descendants. The feature was designed specifically to allow the processors to run several different applications and arbitrate among their demands for hardware resources.

Windows is not the first PC environment to offer multitasking—utilities such as DESQview have provided it for DOS-based programs—and the way programs are multitasked in the most commonly used versions of Windows is not perfect. The multitasking found in Windows 3.1 is *cooperative multitasking*, which means simply that Windows applications have to agree to participate. One ill-behaved program can still hog the processor's time or crash the system. Operating systems such as OS/2 and Windows NT—a version of Windows more focused on a networking environment—have *preemptive multitasking*, in which applications have no choice but to share processing time.

If the multitasking provided by Windows 3.1 is not the first or the best to be found, it is the most significant because of the sheer popularity of Windows 3.1. In many cases, just the ability to switch effortlessly among programs is more important than being able to run programs in the background. Once you've become used to that ability, you can't work without it.

We'll look here at how Windows, running on a PC with a 386 or later processor, uses protected mode, divides memory and processor time among multiple applications, and resolves the applications' conflicting requests for the use of hardware components.

How Windows Runs More Than One Program at Once

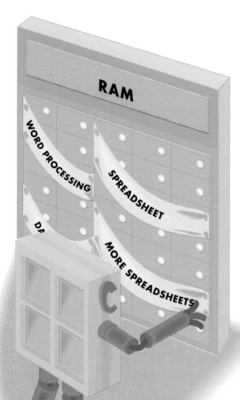

1 As each application is loaded, the processor allocates, from a common pool of all available RAM, a chunk of memory for the exclusive use of that application.

2 If an application needs more memory when it's running, it sends a request to Windows, which checks to see how much memory is available and assigns an additional free stretch of memory to that application.

3 If there isn't enough unallocated memory to match the application's request, Windows checks a table that lists the chunks of memory that have been used most recently. In what is called *virtual memory allocation*, it copies to disk the section of memory that has been used least recently, de-allocates that memory from the program that has been using it, and assigns the memory to the new request.

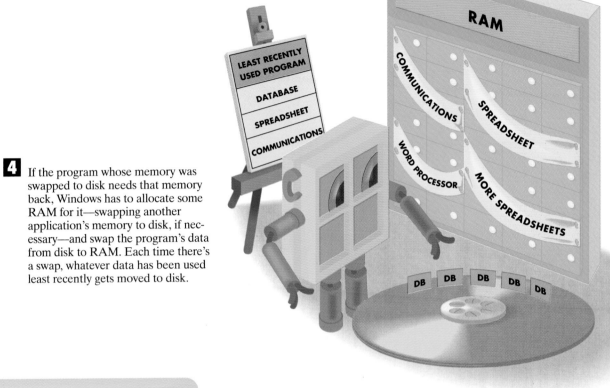

4 If the program whose memory was swapped to disk needs that memory back, Windows has to allocate some RAM for it—swapping another application's memory to disk, if necessary—and swap the program's data from disk to RAM. Each time there's a swap, whatever data has been used least recently gets moved to disk.

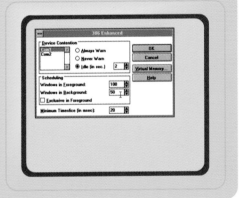

5 When a DOS application is running under Windows, a setting in the Windows Control Panel determines how much processing time should be devoted to Windows applications when a Windows program is in the foreground and when a DOS application is in the foreground.

6 If, for example, the foreground is set to 100 and background is set to 50, all Windows programs will have access to 100 time slices, and each DOS application will use 50 time slices. If three Windows programs and one DOS application were running, two-thirds of the processing time would be divided among the Windows programs. The one DOS program would get one-third of the processor's attention.

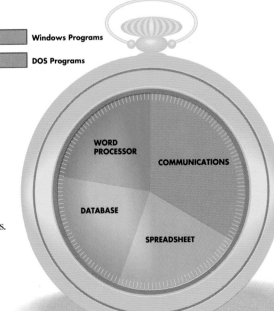

How Windows Lets Programs Share Processing Time

1 To multitask all the programs that are loaded into memory, Windows sends the processor a command that tells it to save the task it's currently performing by writing the contents of the processor's registers to RAM and to make a notation of where in memory it left off processing the program's code.

2 The processor then clears the registers, loads into them the data from the next program, and begins executing that program's instructions from a new location in RAM until the program's time slice expires. Then Windows tells the processor to save those registers and repeat the process for the next application being multitasked.

3 If a program requests a service from hardware—such as using a serial or printer port or drawing something on screen—the request is intercepted by Windows, which checks to see if the same hardware service is being used by another multitasked program.

HARDWARE IN USE

PRINTER PORT ✓
COM PORT
KEYBOARD
MOUSE ✓
RAM
VIDEO

4 If the hardware service is in use, Windows puts the new request into a queue, where it remains until the current hardware operation is completed. Then Windows gives the requesting program access to the hardware through drivers or the BIOS. (An ill-behaved Windows program may try to access hardware directly, without obeying Windows's rules; if that happens, the request may cause Windows to crash.)

QUEUE

5 If a program tries to do something that Windows does not understand—such as dividing by zero or writing to an area of RAM that doesn't belong to it—Windows produces a *general protection fault*. It shuts down the offending application, but protects other multi-tasked programs from crashing—usually.

$100 \div 0$

CLOSED: GENERAL PROTECTION FAULT

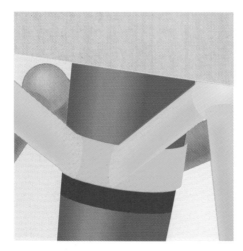

How Windows Shares Program Code

ONE OF THE most brilliant features of Windows is one that you never see directly. It's the modularity that's built into Windows—and because of it, all the Windows programs you use behave more similarly that any selection of DOS programs could ever do. Once you learn one Windows program, you've learned half of everything you need to know to use any other Windows program.

Windows does this by allowing programmers to write software that is modular; any single Windows application actually comprises many files containing code that can be reused in different situations. Even more important, Windows itself provides many of the modules that programs need to perform common functions. For the programmer, this means that there are large chunks of code the programmer doesn't have to create.

You, of course, probably couldn't care less how much work some anonymous programmer has to do. But you're still a beneficiary of this programming method, in two ways. First, because programmers can create new or revised software faster, you don't have to wait as long for revisions of your favorite software. This means it takes less time to get your hands on software that improves how you work. Second, the Windows-supplied modules let different programs from different software companies work similarly. This means you don't have to relearn the most common operations, such as how to open and save files, search for text, or print files.

This is the theory of modularity, and in most cases, it works in practice. But you'll probably always encounter programs written by people convinced they know a "better" way to make a program perform a function. In some cases, they may be right; for example, the Open File dialog box in WordPerfect for Windows provides features for deleting, moving, renaming, and finding files, and creating and removing directories—features not included in Windows's own module function for opening files. The trade-off is that WordPerfect's Open File function is inconsistent in minor ways with a standard Windows Open File box.

Modularity is a mixed blessing. At its best, it makes more programs easier to use. At its worst, it imposes a lowest common denominator that discourages individual brilliance in programming. Overall, ease of use wins out. There are too many instances in which individual programmers have created oddball interfaces that spring more from their personal idiosyncrasies than from brilliance. When an interface is both different *and* truly an improvement, such as WordPerfect's Open File box, the slight deviation from the norm is worth the extra effort of learning it. And such improvements in rival programs just might be noticed by Windows's programmers at Microsoft, and incorporated into future editions of Windows.

In this chapter, we'll look at the most common way in which Windows programs share code—*dynamic link library* (DLL) files. These files normally contain several software routines that can be called upon by other programs. The most commonly used DLLs are those that come with Windows, but most Windows applications come with their own DLLs that contain code used by different features within the applications. If you do your own programming or even advanced macro writing, you can incorporate the routines of both Windows DLLs and application DLLs into your own code.

How Different Windows Programs Use the Same Code

1 When a Windows application wants to use a common function contained in a DLL file, it sends a message to Windows that gives the name of the DLL file, along with the name of the particular function. This procedure is known as *calling* a function. One of the most frequently used DLLs is Windows's COMMDLG.DLL, which includes, among others, the functions to display File Open, File Save, Search, and Print dialog boxes.

CALL COMMDLG.DLL OPEN FILE FUNCTION

RETURN FILE OR

US... FILE.SPEC... *.DOC

2 The application usually also sends any information that the DLL function will need to complete its operation successfully. For example, a program calling the Open File function in Windows's COMMDLG.DLL would pass along a file spec, such as *.* or *.DOC, to be displayed in the dialog box's Filename text box.

3 The application also passes along a specification for the type of information it expects the DLL to send back to the application when the DLL's done its job. The application, for example, may expect return information in the form of integers, true/false values, or text.

4 Windows passes the responsibility for program execution to the DLL, along with the parameters and return information that the DLL needs.

COMMDLG.DLL

5 The specific routine in the DLL is loaded into memory, and then executed by the processor. At this point, the DLL, rather than the application, is running things. It performs all the operations necessary to communicate with Windows and, through it, the operating system and hardware.

6 After the DLL function is complete, the DLL puts the return information into memory, where it can be found by the application, and instructs Windows to remove the DLL function from memory.

7 The application inspects the return information—which usually tells whether the DLL function was able to execute correctly. If the operation was a success, the application continues from where it left off before issuing the function call. If the operation failed, the application displays an error message.

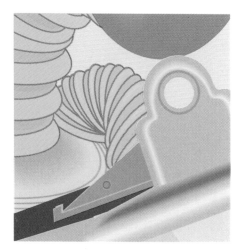

How Windows Shares Data

THEY HAVEN'T YET made a cooking pan that's perfect for both frying chicken and baking angel food cake. Instead, your kitchen contains a collection of pots, pans, bowls, and trays, each best for a certain type of cooking. The same is true of software applications. Each type of application—word processing, spreadsheet, drawing—works best with a specific type of data. There are a few *integrated programs* that combine word processor, spreadsheet, communications, and database management, but their components are never as powerful as stand-alone programs.

And yet data rarely lives in only one program. The graph created by a spreadsheet winds up as part of a graphic presentation. The lists of parts in a database becomes a published catalog. The memo written in a word processor is included in an electronic mail message.

Windows provides several neat, compact solutions to the problem of sharing data among various applications. The Windows *Clipboard* allows you to select a block of text or a graphic in one application, copy it, and paste it into another location in the same application or into a different application altogether. *Dynamic data exchange* (DDE) allows one application to include data created by another application and maintains a live link to that data; that is, the data changes if the original is changed.

Object linking and embedding (OLE) is quickly replacing DDE. Like DDE, OLE allows you to create a live link to data created in a different program. But unlike cut-and-paste or DDE, in which the receiving application changes the format of the pasted information, embedded documents retain all their original properties. OLE lets you click on the embedded data to access the program that created it, so you can modify the data. There are two versions of OLE. Version 1.0 launches the program that created the data and makes it the active foreground application. OLE 2.0 carries the integration one step further. When you double-click on an OLE 2.0 object, the menus and tools of the current application are automatically replaced by those of the application that created the linked data. In effect, OLE 2.0 blends two programs into a single, more powerful program.

Although DDE and OLE 1.0 are outmoded, you'll still find many Windows applications that use them, so we'll look at those features along with the Clipboard and OLE 2.0. Each of these methods is used by Windows to share data among applications, allowing you to work in one large, seamless environment.

How the Windows Clipboard Works

RAM

It was a movie career that began with the four brothers converting their stage comedies into film. **The Marx Bros. are best remembered for *A Night at the Opera*.** But they also created several other musical comedies that will endure as classics.

1 When you select data in an application and either cut or copy it, Windows copies the data to a section of memory reserved for its Clipboard.

NATIVE

OEM   RTF

CHART: PIE
TITLE: SALES

WIDGETS:		110°
GIZMOS:		100°
THINGIES:		20°
STUFF:		130°

DRAWING INSTRUCTIONS

BITMAP   METAFILE   NATIVE

2 The application transfers the selection to Clipboard memory in multiple formats so that you can transfer information among applications that use different formats. Text is stored in three formats. One is the format of the application that created the data. The second is a translation of the application's formatting codes for boldfacing, justification, fonts, and so on into a generic form called *rich text format* (RTF), which is recognized by all Windows applications. The third format is called *OEM* (original equipment manufacturer) text, which is used to paste text into DOS applications.

3 If the data being copied to the Clipboard is a graphic, Windows saves it in three formats—the graphic's original format, such as .TIF or .PCX; a bitmap format; and a *metafile* format. A bitmap is a record of the specific pattern of display pixels that need to be turned on to re-create the image in its original size (see Chapter 15). A metafile is a collection of commands that can be used by Windows's graphic device interface (GDI) to recreate the image (see Chapter 19 for more information about GDI). Metafiles are resolution-independent; that is, they aren't locked into a specific array of pixels, as a bitmap is. This lets metafiles take advantage of all the resolution your display or printer can provide, and it lets you easily resize, or scale, images without distorting them. (A metafile often is called an object-oriented graphic because it is stored as a series of distinct objects—lines, rectangles, arcs—rather than as a map of bits. See Chapter 16.)

4 When you paste data from the Clipboard, the application receiving the data inspects the various formats in which the data is stored on the Clipboard. If you are pasting data into the application from which it was copied, the application will choose its native format.

5 If you are pasting from one application into another, the receiving application will inspect all the formats to find which, of those it understands, maintains the most formatting information. For example, a metafile graphic is preferable to a bit-mapped graphic, because a metafile contains more detailed information that the receiving application can use to change the graphic's size or orientation.

6 To paste data that is in a format other than its native one, the receiving application translates any data that helps define the format of the data—such as boldfacing or fonts—into the formatting codes it uses. If it is receiving a metafile graphic, the application sends the commands contained in the Clipboard to Windows's GDI, which in turn sends the display driver the information the driver needs to create the graphic on screen.

How Dynamic Data Exchange Works

1 Dynamic data exchange requires two Windows applications that both support DDE. The one that requests data is called the *client*. The application that provides the data is called the *server*.

SERVER

DDE

CLIENT

BUDGETS.XLS
RANGE: 1994
APPLICATION:
EXCEL

2 When you create a DDE link between two applications—for example, a word processor client and a spreadsheet server—Windows embeds in the word processor document invisible information that identifies the spreadsheet file, the range to be embedded, and the application that created the file.

3 A DDE link can be set up so that it is updated manually or automatically whenever the client file containing the link is loaded. In either instance, the client sends a message to Windows to update the data from the server to reflect any changes that may have been made in the spreadsheet range since the word processor file was last loaded.

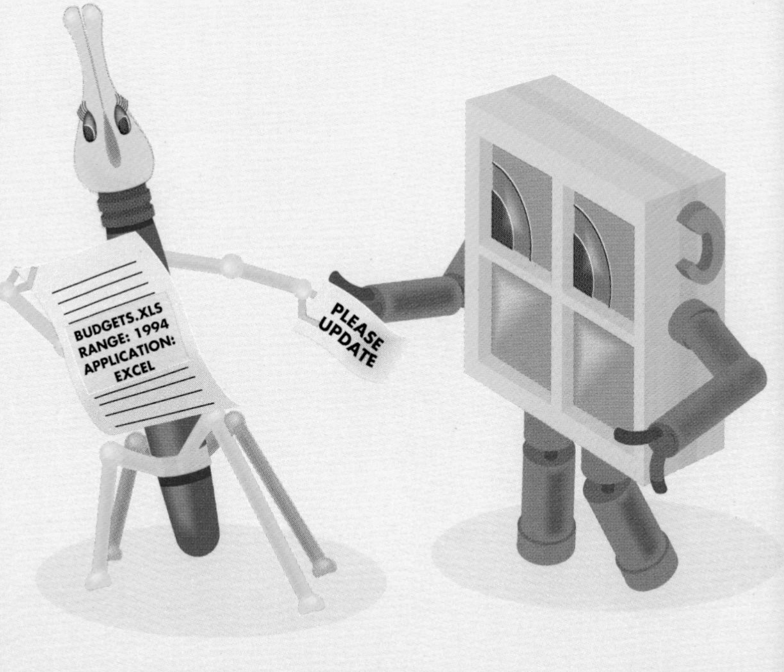

BUDGETS.XLS
RANGE: 1994
APPLICATION:
EXCEL

PLEASE
UPDATE

4 In turn, Windows loads a function contained in the dynamic link library DDEML.DLL, which is dedicated to DDE management. (See Chapter 21 for more information on DLLs.)

5 DDEML.DLL's function checks to see if the server application is already running, either in another window or as an icon. If it isn't, DDEML launches the server application, which loads the file that contains the linked data.

6 The linked information in the server file is copied to the area of memory that contains the file loaded by the client application and replaces the older version of the data.

How Object Linking and Embedding (OLE) 1.0 Works

1 When setting up an OLE link—for example, to a graph from a spreadsheet program—you first copy the graph from the server application. This sends the selection to the Clipboard in several formats—bitmap, metafile, and native (such as .XLS for Excel). It also sends an OLE marker called a *link*.

2 In the application in which you want to include the data— the client application—you choose the OLE paste command (Paste Special, Paste Link, or another variant, depending on the application). This command sends a call to a function in the DLL file OLECLI.DLL, which in turn searches the Clipboard for the link marker. When the OLECLI.DLL function finds the link, it uses it to identify the application that created the data— the server application. The function sends a request, using the same commands employed by DDE, to another DLL, OLESVR.DLL, to create a link between the server application and the client's file.

3 Making the link takes two steps: The data is pasted from the Clipboard to the client application's file, and the client application's paste operation attaches reminders, one for the server application and one for the client.

4 The server file's reminder tells the server application to contact the OLE libraries anytime someone modifies, renames, or saves the data that has been pasted into the client document. If the client application is loaded, the server updates the data. The client file's reminder tells that application to alert the OLE libraries whenever the file is opened. If the server file's data has changed, the client file also changes. [*Continued on next page.*]

How Object Linking and Embedding (OLE) 1.0 Works

5 If an object is embedded rather than linked, there is a reminder that identifies the server application. Objects that are simply linked are updated automatically whenever the data is updated in the server application. Embedding lets you launch the server application by double-clicking on the embedded object.

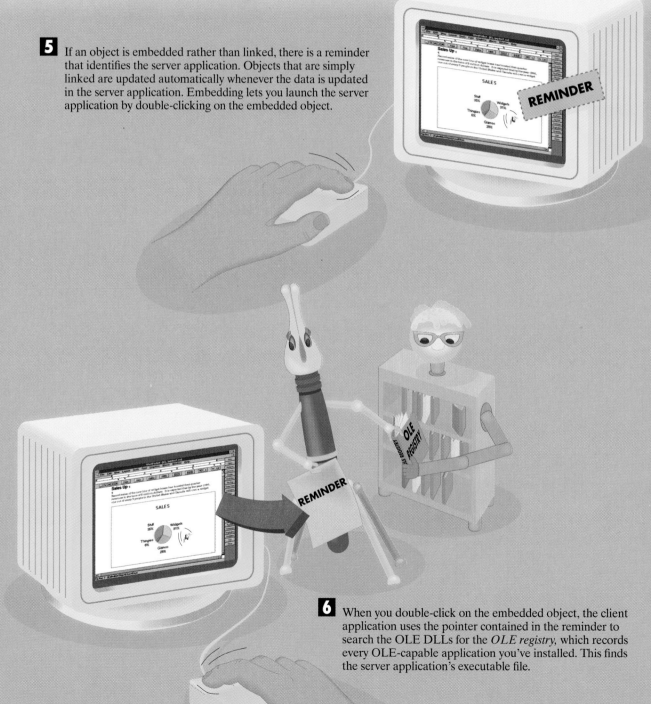

6 When you double-click on the embedded object, the client application uses the pointer contained in the reminder to search the OLE DLLs for the *OLE registry*, which records every OLE-capable application you've installed. This finds the server application's executable file.

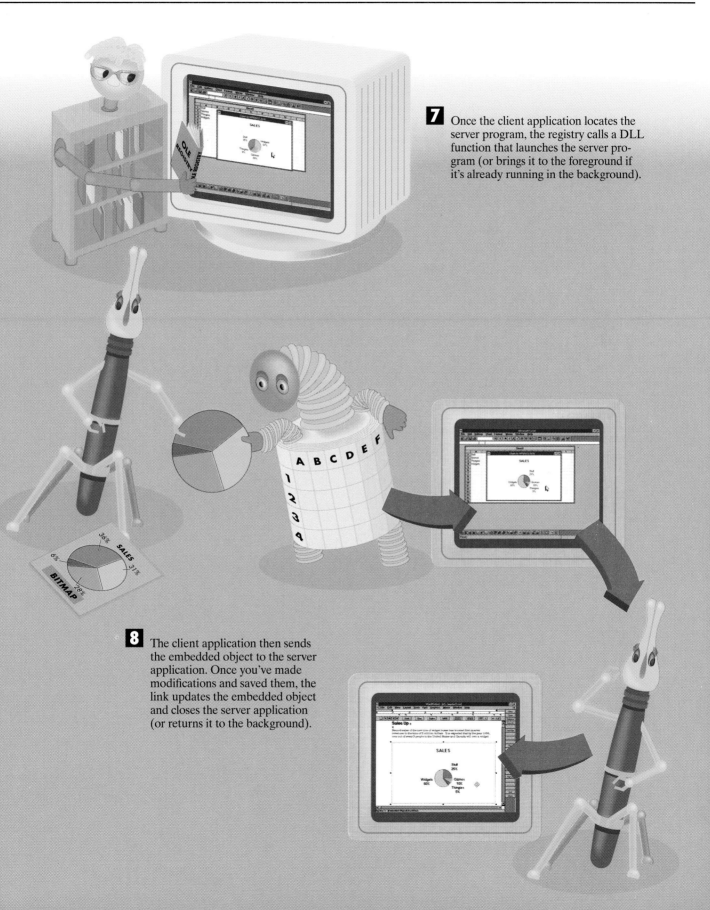

7 Once the client application locates the server program, the registry calls a DLL function that launches the server program (or brings it to the foreground if it's already running in the background).

8 The client application then sends the embedded object to the server application. Once you've made modifications and saved them, the link updates the embedded object and closes the server application (or returns it to the background).

How Object Linking and Embedding (OLE) 2.0 Works

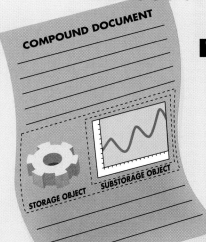

 The process of creating an OLE 2.0 object is similar to that found in OLE 1.0, except that under OLE 2.0, data files can have a more complex structure. In these *compound documents* you can have *storage objects,* a new form of embedded object, that can include their own substorage objects. These data objects include more information about the nature of the objects than is ordinarily provided with a Clipboard link. In effect, they let you embed an object within another embedded object with a more elaborate system of reminders to maintain a record of all the links and server applications.

2 When you double-click on an OLE 2.0 object, the client application inspects the reminders embedded with the object to identify the application that created the object.

3 The client application sends a message to an OLE DLL, telling the DLL that the client needs the functions of the server application to work with the object.

4 The DLL passes the request to the application, which in turn calls on another DLL routine that activates functions in USER.EXE, the Windows module responsible for handling Windows menus. (See Chapter 19.)

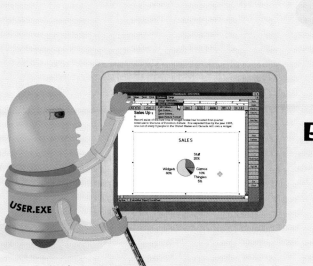

5 USER.EXE replaces some of the menus in the client application with menus from the server application. The client retains the more generic File and Window menus, but the other menus, which typically involve features unique to a specific application, are replaced.

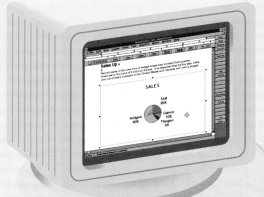

6 Using the substitute menu items, you can modify the embedded object just as if you were in the server application itself. Clicking outside the embedded object restores the client application's own menus.

records. *See also* databases
    defined, 71
    fixed- vs. variable-length,
      74, 75
registers, 8, 47, 50–51
relational databases, 69, 83–87
relative address, 8
reverse Polish notation, 100
rich text format, 184
RLE, 133
ROM
    and BIOS, 14
    chips, 118
routines, 45, 65
rows. *See* spreadsheets
RTF, 184
run-length encoding, 133

S

screens, display drivers, 108, 111,
    113
searching. *See* databases
segment address, 8
segmentation unit, 11
segmented memory, 6, 8–9
segment registers, 47
shapes. *See* graphics software
software. *See also particular*
    software type
    application vs. system, 19
    modularity of, 177–178
    translating ideas into, 53–57
sorting. *See* databases
source code, 60
sparse matrix, 93
spreadsheets
    data storage in, 93–97
    formulas used in, 99–101
    overview, 90–91

start bits, 146, 150
stop bits, 146, 150
storage objects, 192
strings, defined, 53
syntax, 53, 63, 65
system events, handling under
    Windows, 168–169
system message queue, 168
system software. *See* operating
    systems

T

telecommunications. *See*
    communications
tokens, 63
transfer protocols, 153–157
transistors, 5
transmission speed, 146, 150
two-dimensional arrays, 93
typefaces. *See also* fonts
    evolution of, 105
    vs. fonts, 115

U

UMBs, 37, 38
upper memory, 33, 36–41

V

variable-length data fields, 72, 75
variables
    defined, 45
    in programs, 53
vector graphics, 135–139
video adapters and BIOS, 14
virtual memory allocation, 172
VisiCalc, 90–91

W

Windows
    and BIOS, 16
    Clipboard, 182, 184–185,
      188–189
    dynamic data exchange,
      186–187
    graphic interface, 163–169
    handling system events,
      168–169
    NT, as operating system, 19–20
    object linking and embedding,
      160, 188–193
    overview, 160
    running multiple sessions,
      171–175
    sharing data, 183
    sharing processing time,
      174–175
    sharing program codes,
      177–181
    and word processors, 107, 108
WordPerfect, 107
word processors
    formatting documents. *See*
      formatting documents
    overview, 104–105

X

X-base databases, 71
Xmodem protocol, 153, 156–157
XMS, 33–34

Y

Ymodem protocol, 153

Z

Zmodem protocol, 153

Attention Teachers and Trainers
Now You Can
Teach From These Books!

ZD Press now offers instructors and trainers
the materials they need to use these books in their classes.

- An Instructor's Manual features flexible lessons designed for use in a
  10- or 15-week course (30-45 course hours).

- Student exercises and tests on floppy disk provide you with an easy way
  to tailor and/or duplicate tests as you need them.

- A Transparency Package contains all the graphics from the book, each on
  a single, full-color transparency.

- Spanish edition of *PC/Computing How Computers Work* will be available.

Imagination. Innovation. Insight.

The How It Works Series from Ziff-Davis Press

"... a magnificently seamless integration of text and graphics ..."

Larry Blasko, The Associated Press, reviewing *PC/Computing How Computers Work*

No other books bring computer technology to life like the *How It Works* series from Ziff-Davis Press. Lavish, full-color illustrations and lucid text from some of the world's top computer commentators make *How It Works* books an exciting way to explore the inner workings of PC technology.

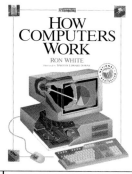

ISBN: 094-7 Price: $22.95

PC/Computing How Computers Work

A worldwide blockbuster that hit the general trade bestseller lists! *PC/Computing* magazine executive editor Ron White dismantles the PC and reveals what really makes it tick.

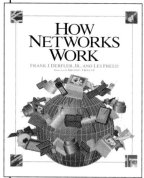

ISBN: 129-3 Price: $24.95

How Networks Work

Two of the most respected names in connectivity showcase the PC network, illustrating and explaining how each component does its magic and how they all fit together.

ISBN: 166-8 Price: $15.95
Available: October

How Macs Work

A fun and fascinating voyage to the heart of the Macintosh! Two noted *MacUser* contributors cover the spectrum of Macintosh operations from startup to shutdown.

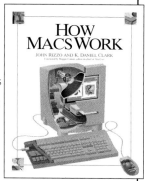

ISBN: 146-3 Price: $24.95

ISBN: 133-1 Price: $24.95
Available: October

How Software Works

This dazzlingly illustrated volume from Ron White peeks inside the PC to show in full-color how software breathes life into the PC. Covers Windows™ and all major software categories.

How to Use Your Computer

Conquer computerphobia and see how this intricate machine truly makes life easier. Dozens of full-color graphics showcase the components of the PC and explain how to interact with them.

All About Computers

This one-of-a-kind visual guide for kids features numerous full-color illustrations and photos on every page, combined with dozens of interactive projects that reinforce computer basics, making this an exciting way to learn all about the world of computers.

ISBN: 155-2 Price: $19.95

© 1993 Ziff-Davis Press

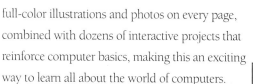

Available at all fine bookstores or by calling 1-800-688-0448, ext. 100. Call for more information on the Instructor's Supplement, including transparencies for each book in the How It Works Series.

Arrrgh!

Don't you just hate it when software doesn't work the way you expect? When simple problems block your progress for hours? When your resident techie isn't around, the technical support hotline is constantly busy, on-line help is no help at all, the manual is hopeless, and the book you have tells you everything except what you really need to know?

Don't you just hate it?

We do too. That's why we developed *HELP!*, a groundbreaking series of books from ZD Press.

HELP! books mean fast access to straight answers. If you're a beginner, you'll appreciate the practical examples and skill-building exercises that will help you work confidently in no time. If you're already an experienced user, you'll love the comprehensive coverage, highly detailed indexes, and margin notes and sidebars that highlight especially helpful information.

We're launching the *HELP!* series with these all-new books:

HELP! WordPerfect 6.0—WordPerfect insider Stephen G. Dyson has created the most complete single source of techniques, examples, and advice that will help you clear the hurdles of WordPerfect 6.0 quickly and easily.

HELP! Microsoft Access—Best-selling author Miriam Liskin gives you fast access to the complete feature set of Microsoft's leading-edge Windows database program. Sample databases included on disk!

HELP! Paradox for Windows—Popular database and spreadsheet authority Lisa Biow provides one-stop solutions to the challenges of Borland's high-powered new database manager.

More *HELP!* is on the way soon for Lotus Notes 3.0, and Windows NT 3.1. So if you hate struggling with software as much as we do, visit your favorite bookstore and just say *HELP!*

ISBN: 1-56276-099-8
Retail Price: $29.95

ISBN: 1-56276-039-4
Retail Price: $27.95

ISBN: 1-56276-014-9
Retail Price: $27.95

Available at all fine bookstores or by calling 1-800-688-0448, ext. 101.

ZIFF-DAVIS
ZD
PRESS

MAXIMIZE YOUR PRODUCTIVITY WITH THE TECHNIQUES & UTILITIES SERIES

Insider Networking Secrets Revealed by Renowned Experts Frank J. Derfler, Jr., and Les Freed

Frank J. Derfler, Jr., and Les Freed have pooled their knowledge to create the most extensive guides to networking and communications. Active in the PC industry since its birth, Freed is the founder of DCA's Crosstalk division, and Derfler is senior networking editor of *PC Magazine* and the writer of the magazine's "Connectivity" column. You can be assured you are learning from highly respected experts in the computer industry with the most up-to-date information available.

With the wisdom of Derfler and Freed, you will boost your network system performance and productivity in no time.

PC Magazine Guide to Windows for Workgroups

ISBN: 120-X
Price: $22.95

Both users and administrators will get up and running fast and enjoy an instant boost in workgroup productivity with the help of this concise, easy-to-read guide.

PC Magazine Guide to NetWare

ISBN: 022-X
Price: $39.95

Les Freed and Frank J. Derfler, Jr. present tips, tricks, and techniques that make this best-selling book/disk package the essential survival guide to NetWare.

PC Magazine Guide to LANtastic

ISBN: 058-0
Price: $19.95

Best-selling authors and networking experts Frank J. Derfler, Jr., and Les Freed show you how to master the full power of LANtastic.

PC Magazine Guide to Connectivity, Second Edition

ISBN: 047-5
Price: $39.95

This supercharged second edition of the connectivity bible from Frank J. Derfler, Jr., includes *PC Magazine*'s most up-to-date product information, plus a special section on modem communication. You'll receive two disks that contain a full-featured e-mail program, performance-testing utilities, and many other application and utility programs.

PC Magazine Guide to Modem Communications

ISBN: 037-8
Price: $29.95

Acclaimed experts Les Freed and Frank J. Derfler, Jr., cover the fundamentals of modem communica-tions, and provide scores of tips and insights on purchasing the right equipment and using bulletin board systems and modems for business applications. A valuable companion disk includes scripts for accessing on-line services, a file compression/decompression utility, and many more time-saving programs.

PC Magazine Guide to Linking LANs

ISBN: 031-9
Price: $39.95

Network authority, Frank J. Derfler, Jr., shows you the most effective ways to share network resources with the LAN down the hall or around the globe. This essential guide gives practical advice on quality, cost, and compatibility for dozens of popular products.

ZIFF-DAVIS ZD PRESS

Available at all fine bookstores, or by calling 1-800-688-0448, ext. 104.

Ziff-Davis Press Survey of Readers

Please help us in our effort to produce the best books on personal computing.
For your assistance, we would be pleased to send you a FREE catalog
featuring the complete line of Ziff-Davis Press books.

1. How did you first learn about this book?

Recommended by a friend . . . . ☐ -1 (5)

Recommended by store personnel . . . . ☐ -2

Saw in Ziff-Davis Press catalog . . . . ☐ -3

Received advertisement in the mail . . . . ☐ -4

Saw the book on bookshelf at store . . . . ☐ -5

Read book review in: _____ ☐ -6

Saw an advertisement in: _____ ☐ -7

Other (Please specify): _____ ☐ -8

2. Which THREE of the following factors most influenced your decision to purchase this book? (Please check up to THREE.)

Front or back cover information on book . . . ☐ -1 (6)

Logo of magazine affiliated with book . . . . . . ☐ -2

Special approach to the content . . . . ☐ -3

Completeness of content . . . . ☐ -4

Author's reputation. ☐ -5

Publisher's reputation . . . . ☐ -6

Book cover design or layout . . . . ☐ -7

Index or table of contents of book . . . . ☐ -8

Price of book . . . . ☐ -9

Special effects, graphics, illustrations . . . . . . ☐ -0

Other (Please specify): _____ ☐ -x

3. How many computer books have you purchased in the last six months? _____ (7-10)

4. On a scale of 1 to 5, where 5 is excellent, 4 is above average, 3 is average, 2 is below average, and 1 is poor, please rate each of the following aspects of this book below. (Please circle your answer.)

Depth/completeness of coverage   5 4 3 2 1 (11)

Organization of material   5 4 3 2 1 (12)

Ease of finding topic   5 4 3 2 1 (13)

Special features/time saving tips   5 4 3 2 1 (14)

Appropriate level of writing   5 4 3 2 1 (15)

Usefulness of table of contents   5 4 3 2 1 (16)

Usefulness of index   5 4 3 2 1 (17)

Usefulness of accompanying disk   5 4 3 2 1 (18)

Usefulness of illustrations/graphics   5 4 3 2 1 (19)

Cover design and attractiveness   5 4 3 2 1 (20)

Overall design and layout of book   5 4 3 2 1 (21)

Overall satisfaction with book   5 4 3 2 1 (22)

5. Which of the following computer publications do you read regularly; that is, 3 out of 4 issues?

Byte . . . . ☐ -1 (23)

Computer Shopper . . . . ☐ -2

Corporate Computing . . . . ☐ -3

Dr. Dobb's Journal . . . . ☐ -4

LAN Magazine . . . . ☐ -5

MacWEEK . . . . ☐ -6

MacUser . . . . ☐ -7

PC Computing . . . . ☐ -8

PC Magazine . . . . ☐ -9

PC WEEK . . . . ☐ -0

Windows Sources . . . . ☐ -x

Other (Please specify): _____ ☐ -y

Please turn page.

6. What is your level of experience with personal computers? With the subject of this book?

	With PCs	With subject of book
Beginner	☐ -1 (24)	☐ -1 (25)
Intermediate	☐ -2	☐ -2
Advanced	☐ -3	☐ -3

7. Which of the following best describes your job title?

Officer (CEO/President/VP/owner)........ ☐ -1 (26)
Director/head......................... ☐ -2
Manager/supervisor................... ☐ -3
Administration/staff.................. ☐ -4
Teacher/educator/trainer............. ☐ -5
Lawyer/doctor/medical professional....... ☐ -6
Engineer/technician.................. ☐ -7
Consultant.......................... ☐ -8
Not employed/student/retired........... ☐ -9
Other (Please specify): _____ ☐ -0

8. What is your age?

Under 20............................. ☐ -1 (27)
21-29............................... ☐ -2
30-39............................... ☐ -3
40-49............................... ☐ -4
50-59............................... ☐ -5
60 or over.......................... ☐ -6

9. Are you:

Male................................ ☐ -1 (28)
Female.............................. ☐ -2

Thank you for your assistance with this important information! Please write your address below to receive our free catalog.

Name: _____

Address: _____

City/State/Zip: _____

Fold here to mail.

1331-13-08

NO POSTAGE
NECESSARY
IF MAILED IN
THE UNITED
STATES

BUSINESS REPLY MAIL
FIRST CLASS MAIL   PERMIT NO. 1612   OAKLAND, CA

POSTAGE WILL BE PAID BY ADDRESSEE

Ziff-Davis Press

5903 Christie Avenue
Emeryville, CA 94608-1925
Attn: Marketing

Cut Here